Little Apples Growing

FLORENCE M. HAMMOND

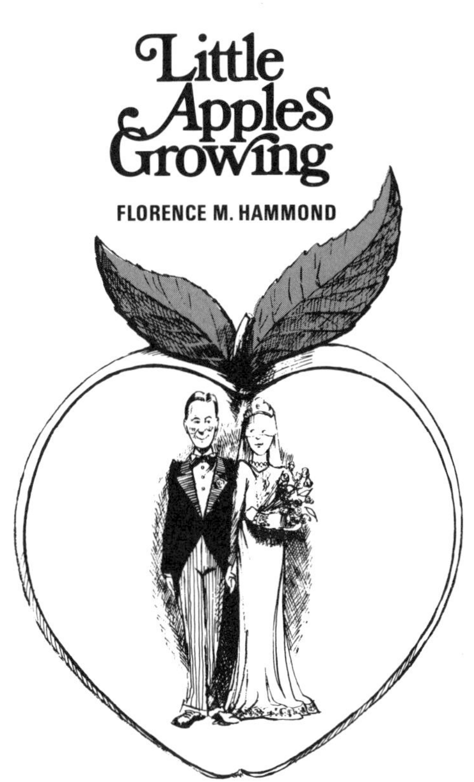

Dedicated to my granddaughters Catherine Mary and Shannon Lynn Freure.

All too soon there comes a time in our lives when we start looking back instead of forward, and the looking back brings joy, a tear or two, and sometimes a thought of "how did we live through it?"

Unlike the "old salt" who takes his grandchild on his knee to tell him stories of his escapades when he sailed the briny deep, my experiences on the somewhat stormy sea of life are recorded in this book so that my grandchildren, Cathy and Shannon Freure, may reflect on them as they relax on the floor with their feet draped over a chair as I have often seen them do.

Chapter I

Romance through Conspiracy.

We met in a savings bank. I was depositing the day's receipts from the law office. Clare was entering the deposit in the passbook. As Lorne Shantz sauntered toward us, he frowned over a piece of paper he held in his hands. Then he raised it close to Clare's face as he ran his finger along it several times. Clare's face sobered as he glared at it and then at his colleague's face. "Oh, Oh!" he gulped. (One year after we were married, I learned that there wasn't a thing written on it!)

"By the way, Clare, meet Miss Ayres, a friend of mine from Clement's Law Office."

"How do you do?" beamed Clare as he handed the passbook to me.

I smiled, blushed, accepted the passbook, turned on my heel and hurried back to my office.

Two days later there was more money to deposit. "Do you mind running over to the bank for me?" questioned the book-keeper. "If you have too much work on your book, I'll go myself."

"Oh, no, I can go!" I blurted. "My work is almost finished!"

Over to the bank I dashed! The cashier accepted the deposit and slipped the passbook through to the ledgerkeeper. He entered it and, as he turned to hand the book back, he said "How'dya like to go to the Bell Telephone dance with me on Friday evening?"

"I'd love to — do you know where I live?"

"Oh, yes, Lorne told me - 72 Wellington Street - I'll pick you up at eight."

The Bell Telephone dance, toboggan parties, house parties, visits to his home near Port Elgin to meet his parents and then, in August of 1928, we were married. Clare changed his job so that he could settle permanently in Kitchener, and I kept on working in the law office.

We rented a two-room apartment at 145 King Street, West, close to our jobs. Each room was about nine feet by twelve, and the bathroom, which we shared with four other families, was down at the end of a long hall.

For the kitchen, we purchased a three-burner gas stove, a kitchen cabinet for dishes, pots and pans, and staple foodstuffs.

The perishable foods like meat, milk and butter were kept in an ice box the top section of which held fifty pounds of ice that melted and trickled down a pipe into a pan concealed underneath it which we had to empty once a day. A table and four chairs, gaily painted in apple green, completed the furnishing of that room.

Since the other room had to serve as both living-room and bedroom, we purchased a chesterbed that reached almost from wall to wall, leaving just enough room to accommodate a small console radio, an easy chair, an end table to stand by it, a table for under the window, a table lamp, a pair of bookends, and a mat.

Before we could go to bed at night, we had to roll up the mat, put the end table on the easy chair, slide them into the kitchen, remove the cushions from the chesterbed, place them on the floor under the table that stood by the window, unfold the chesterbed, get the pillows, sheets and blankets from a box underneath the kitchen cabinet, make the bed and crawl in. Then Clare would flip the radio off with his toe.

Next morning, we would crawl out of bed at six-thirty, put the blankets, sheets and pillows back in the box beneath the kitchen cabinet, fold up the chesterbed, replace the cushions that were under the table that stood by the window, slide the easy chair and end table back into the living-room, put the end table in its place and unroll the mat! That left room to pull our chairs from under the kitchen table so that we could eat breakfast before we slid off to work for a nine o'clock start.

One Friday evening, Clare said he would like some homemade tea biscuits "like his mother used to make". Armed with a cookbook, I read the recipe, got out all the ingredients and mixed up a batch. When they came out of the oven, my ever-loving husband snatched one, and tried to sink his teeth into it.

"Boy, oh, boy, if we had enough of these, we could build a house with them."

Heartbroken, I flopped on the chesterbed and cried my eyes out. Every nail in the wall seemed to echo those words — "If we had enough of these, we could build a house with them."

The next day being Saturday, we worked in our offices until noon. At five o'clock, we boarded the train for Paisley to visit Clare's parents on the farm near Dobbinton. It was almost eleven p.m. when we arrived at the farm and as we sat with them enjoying a late lunch of tender, fluffy tea biscuits, maple syrup, and tea,

I told them we were going to build a house! The look of surprise on their faces bespoke their thoughts that perhaps we had won a sweepstake or robbed a bank!

"Yes, I made biscuits last night, and Clare said, 'If we had enough of these, we could build a house', and I cried myself to sleep."

As Mother Hammond slipped to the stove to put more hot water into the teapot, Clare's father whispered, "Put more shortening in, Florence, that's what makes them tender, and Mother makes them with pure cream if she has some on hand."

"O.K. He won't be able to build a house with the next ones," I whispered back to him. "They'll melt in his mouth!"

Mother returned from the stove with the teapot and as she poured another round she grinned as she started to tell us about Uncle Jim giving Janet Darrow a ride to town in his new car.

I had met Janet one time when Clare's folks gave her a ride to town. She was six feet, two inches tall, and as broad as a barn door. Her complexion was ruddy and she had muscles like balloons. Her ankle-length skirts swirled around her as she chewed up the five-mile distance to town with her feet clad in men's bush boots.

According to Mother, Uncle Jim picked her up as she was starting out. She got in the car, slammed the door, talked a blue streak the whole distance and when they arrived at their destination, Uncle Jim stopped to let her out. As she set her feet on the ground, she swung around, slammed the door of the car, shattering the glass which ran down on the road like peas.

"Oh! Oh! You can putty it, James!" she said, as she headed for the bank with her bulging purse.

We had just recovered from our laughter enough to put a bite into our mouths when Brother Frank said, "Tell them about the butter!"

"Oh, yes. Several of us went to help with a threshing at Janet's place last summer and she lugged a huge crock of butter from the cellar, placed it on the side-table, and when we took the cover off, it nearly knocked us over. When we buttered the bread for dinner, spreading it as thin as possible, Janet came over and said, "Slash 'er on, folks! There's lots of 'er!"

We finished our late lunch, helped clear the table, stacked the dishes to be washed with the breakfast ones next morning, and made our way upstairs to bed behind Mother, whose face was still a bit green from talking about Janet's butter.

We awoke next morning to the sound of the rooster making his importance known to his barnyard companions, and went downstairs to partake of the usual farm breakfast. The table was laden with cereals, meat, fried potatoes, tea biscuits, maple syrup, honey, jam, apple pie, and piles of toast that Dad Hammond had made over the red-hot coals in the cook stove.

After breakfast, the men left for the barn to do their chores while we women cleaned up the table and washed the dishes from breakfast as well as the ones from our midnight lunch. Later in the day, the folks drove us to Paisley to catch the train for Kitchener. "Must get home early, both gotta work tomorrow," Clare reminded his parents as we pulled away.

Chapter II

The Vale of Tears

It was the first deed and mortgage that I saw in Business College which prompted my desire to work in a law office. By the time we were married, I had had three years' experience with the firm of Clement, Hattin & Snider. The office was above the Waterloo Trust and Savings Company at the corner of King and Ontario Streets.

Life in a law office is never dull. "Work here for fifty years and there is something new every day," Rubie Fisher would say.

A law secretary's life is a continuous round of letters, wills, writs, deeds, mortgages and descriptions of properties. As you flip out descriptions in rods, chains and minutes north, south, east or west, you direct a client into your boss's office.

He greets the client, shuts the door, it opens again, he comes toward you almost on the run and whispers, "Florence, what is the name of that man in my office?"

You answer, "He's from Windsor - that's Mr. Beck. Remember, he had trouble with his property on Samuel Street?"

He rushes back into his office, a paper in hand as a cover-up, the door closes behind him, your brain starts to twirl again on those rods, chains and minutes, and your fingers obey the command of that brain.

Often a client's face foretells his mission. A smiling face might tell us he had won his case and was receiving the settlement, or, perhaps, that he had sold his property at a profit and wanted a deed drawn. If he was there to make his will, his face might have that order-my-coffin look. Sometimes a sad face depicted bereavement, if clients were dressed in black - the older ones, that is. The young folks didn't believe in dressing in black, or perhaps the one who died had told them not to as my father did. "If you dress in black when I die, I'll haunt you," he would say.

If a client's face was red, his mouth set, and he fidgeted in the waiting room chair, you could depend on it he either had had a fight with his wife and wanted a divorce, or that his brother was willed the lion's share of his father's estate and he was there to start proceedings to break the will.

Then there was the client who was charged with the theft of tires from a local service station. He came in at one-thirty just as I returned from lunch. I told him Mr. Hattin would be in immediately and asked him to have a chair. Since our desks were around the corner of the L-shaped office, we couldn't see the waiting room while we were working. As I typed away a noise of metal rattling reached my ears. It sounded like the combination of the vault. I didn't dare stop typing or he would know I heard it, and so I simply typed slower and, sure enough, he was tampering with the combination. I kept on typing, he kept on tampering! Then the noise stopped! Then Mr. Hattin's secretary, Hilda Hamel, came in. She took her place at her desk beside me and when she started to type, I wrote on a piece of paper, "That fellow was tampering with the combination of our vault." I held the note above her typewriter so that she could read it. When Mr. Hattin came in Miss Hamel went into his office behind him and showed him the note. He called the young man into his office, gave him a calling down, refused to act for him, and requested him to leave. After he left, the combination of the vault was changed.

Later on, the Waterloo Trust expanded its business and our office moved to the second floor of the Bank of Toronto Building in the block between Queen and Benton Streets. There was no elevator and the steps to the second floor seemed endless and steep, but every morning at nine o'clock and every afternoon about two, Mr. W. P. Clement would run up those steps two at a time, and when he went out of the office, he would run down them two at a time.

One day in the fall of 1929, Rubie Fisher, Beulah Koehler, and I were working away at our typewriters. We could hear the pounding on the steps. We knew who was coming! Nobody else could take those steps at that rate! Mr. W. P. (We called him that to distinguish him from Mr. E. W. Clement) came in. As he headed for his private office, he swung his head in our direction as he always did when he said "Good morning", but this time he blurted — "The stock market crashed!"

We looked at him wide-eyed and then at each other! "What does that mean?" I questioned. Miss Fisher drawled, "That - will - be - bad - for - business."

The four members of the firm gathered in one of the private offices to discuss the bad news. We resumed our work pounding out those shorthand notes as if they might be the last we would get!

An hour later each man went to his private office and one after the other the buzzers calling us for dictation sounded. The morning passed quickly and the first one to flit by my desk to go for lunch was Mr. E. W. "Going home to see what the neighbours have brought in," he quipped. "Have an early appointment after lunch, be back at one-thirty."

As we hurried back to our office, here and there groups of people with gloomy faces congregated and snatches of their conversations told us the stock market crash was on the tip of everybody's tongue. Back in the office, every client lamented the event. At home in the evening special newscasts on the radio hummed with it. Broadcasters gave their opinions on its implications, and soon we felt the sting of those implications.

Chapter III

It Struck Home.

At the time of the stock market crash, Clare was working in the Canadian Goodrich Office. One morning in late August the following year, he was preparing for work. He went to the bathroom to shave and when he returned I thought he looked rather strange! As I studied his face, he started to laugh and I realized he had shaved off his mustache.

"Oh, my gosh. You didn't shave off your mustache! My mother told me every time Dad shaved off his mustache, the sky fell in on them! I hope that doesn't happen to us!"

Sure enough, in September, the firm laid off twenty-two of their office staff and he was one of them. He pounded the pavement for one month and secured a job in the office of the Mayfair Hotel owned by the late Mr. Edward Lippert, Sr. When he prepared for work each morning, he carefully shaved around his upper lip and soon that lucky old cookie duster appeared again!

"If this job does well, perhaps we will be able to get a bigger apartment. Rather inconvenient when the folks come down from the farm," he said one morning. "There's three of them and two of us." By the time you put half the furniture in the hall, open up the chesterfield in the living-room, lay their feather bed down on the kitchen floor for them to sleep on, everything is wall-to-wall including the people."

The folks arrived about noon, Mother Hammond, Frank and his girl friend, loaded down with a feather bed, a crate of eggs, a jar of fruit, a jar of pickles, and a pint of cream. Farm cream - not city cream!

We stuffed the feather bed behind the chesterfield, the overnight bags under the kitchen table, the crate of eggs outside the door in the main hall, the fruit, pickles, and cream in the ice box. We women prepared dinner in the kitchen while the men slipped down to Loblaw's King Street, West, just below our apartment, to sell the crate of eggs.

"Farm prices have dropped since the stock crash. Bet he won't get much for those eggs," Mother Hammond lamented.

Soon they were back. "A dollar, forty-four for twelve dozen

eggs," said Frank. "Twelve cents a dozen isn't even enough to pay the feed. Might as well go out of chickens."

Late Sunday our guests left for home and we prepared for the busy week ahead.

The old adage about "blue Monday" was often shattered in the office of Clement, Hattin & Snider, with such things as twisted names and addresses. This Monday was no exception. Opening the mail was our first duty of the day. The envelopes were carefully checked so that no personal mail was opened. These were only slit for the convenience of the receiver. The general mail was opened and placed in piles to be distributed to the various members of the firm. As I picked up the last letter, my eyes fell on the name "Messrs. Clement, Hobbin & Sinder."

Another Monday morning, not long after that, Mr. Hattin, who was very tall and thin, came out of his private office with a letter in his hand, grinning from ear to ear, and said, "I know I'm thin, but I didn't think it was this bad. This letter starts off, "Dear Mr. Hatpin."

Then there was the day when Mr. E. W. Clement informed us he was going to England with a client on a business trip. "There will be a lot of work to clean up in the next three weeks before I leave. Guess I will have to use the dictaphone so you can work on some of it while I'm away, Florence." (He had never used a dictaphone before.)

He dictated the regular daily letters and documents to me and while I transcribed that work he dictated away to the dictaphone. He even went back in the evening and worked till all hours to have everything shipshape for his clients while he was away.

Four days before he was to leave for England, he handed me the last of the completed files to return to the filing cabinet. With a complacent smile and a big sigh, he relaxed in his swivel chair, folded his arms, and proceeded to tell me a little about the trip he was taking. When I went back to my typewriter, the ten cylinders he had dictated were lined up on my desk.

Now ten dictaphone records can represent a lot of work, especially in a law office where documents must sometimes be prepared to go with the letters, and since I had finished the work on my book, I decided to start on the cylinders.

I put the cylinder on the machine, the earphones over my ears, and listened for the first item so that I could put the correct paper in my typewriter; all I could hear was "whooooo — ch - ch - ch - ch." I listened again and again, moved the needle down to another part of the record, and all it said was "ch - ch - ch - ch - ch."

I told Rubie Fisher, she listened, and heard the same thing - only the scratching of the needle on the record! Beulah Koehler took a turn and the same thing happened. We tried other records and on a few, we could hear a voice away in the distance, but not clear enough to make it out.

In desperation, I went into Mr. E. W.'s office and told him we couldn't make out one word on the dictaphone records! He came to the outer office and listened but he couldn't hear anything either.

Mr. Hattin heard the commotion, came over to see what the trouble was and when we told him, he said, "Oh, yes, I know what happened. You didn't talk right into the speaking tube at all times. You can't reach over your desk for papers and turn your head away from the speaking tube or it will not register. I've had that experience a few times. You must speak directly into the tube."

All the papers had been replaced in the files each day as he was finished with them and he had torn up the rough notes he had used as reminders during that three weeks of preparation for his trip, and he looked as dejected as a prospective bridegroom left standing at the altar.

He returned to his private office and sat down at his desk for ten minutes or so. Then he buzzed for me to bring in my book for dictation.

"I'll dictate the most important things and the rest will have to wait until I return."

For three days, morning, afternoon, and evening, he dictated reams and reams of shorthand till I had an acute case of writer's cramp, a pain-racked spine, a mental block, and his voice was down to an incoherent rasp.

"Life is never dull in a Law Office," he said. "Let's get out of this Vale of Tears."

Later that evening, when our chatter about the blank dictaphone records subsided, our conversation turned to that "bigger apartment" Clare said we might get if his work went well. Things did seem to be going very well. His work at the Mayfair Hotel brought him in contact with many business men and he met the manager of the Consolidated Felt Company, who offered him a position in their office at a much better salary.

We moved into a three-room apartment on Benton Street above the Rosedale Creamery. Here we had a living-room, kitchen, an honest-to-goodnses bedroom, and a private bathroom. We purchased a new bedroom suite - no more opening of chesterbeds or wall-to-wall visitors sleeping on a feather bed in the kitchen! Things were beginning to look mighty uppity to us!

Then September came! The fifteenth was Clare's pay day. He pulled a cheque from his envelope and there was a pink slip attached to it! He read it aloud — "Due to the decline in business, your services are no longer required."

We looked at each other but neither of us spoke for several minutes and then I said, "Oh, well, I still have my job. I can carry on until you get something. September doesn't seem to be our lucky month! At least you didn't shave your mustache off this time!"

He turned, edged toward the window, and I got a side-view of his face! I ran over to him, swung him around toward me and sure enough, his face was clean-shaven!

"Now maybe you'll believe me! Don't ever shave that mustache off again. It's bad luck!"

He had two weeks' notice to work out and during that time he learned the company was moving back to Montreal and would be taking with them only the few employees who came with them when they moved to Kitchener a few years before.

Pavement pounding started again. Early every morning he went out, called on one business after the other, got nothing but a laugh in his face, returned home at five-thirty discouraged and almost too tired to eat.

One evening when he came in, he said, "I met Fred Hammond today (Fred was his second cousin) and he suggested I take up barbering. He said he's busy enough. People will always need a haircut."

"How much will that cost?" I enquired.

"Fred said about a hundred and twenty-five dollars with the tools."

"Well, I have my last hundred dollar bonus from Clement's Office in the bank. You can have that. I think we can rake up enough for the tools too."

Rake it up we did and Clare went to the Barber College on Queen Street, South, to take the three months' course. He liked the work, and successfully completed the course despite the fact that he once almost cut a man's throat when he was shaving him.

Pavement pounding! Pavemount pounding! It started again! Try as he liked, he couldn't get a job in a barber shop. "Business is slipping off — can handle it by myself," they would say.

"Well, if they're making a living, so can I," Clare said one morning as he rushed out of the apartment. Later on he came back and informed me he had rented a shop on Queen Street, South, near the barber college where he took his course, and was open for business the next morning.

Thirty days later, the business was bankrupt and our bank account had only eighty-nine cents on the laughing side.

Yes, it struck home, and it struck our friends' homes. Many of them were out of work and on City relief. The words Rubie Fisher said the day Mr. W. P. told us the stock market crashed, rang in my ears many times. "It - will - be - bad - for business."

Chapter IV

It Pays To Advertise

Every day Clare trudged from business to business, and every evening we scanned the help wanted ads in the newspaper. White collar workers' jobs were scarce as hen's teeth, and then one night he noticed that the Twin City Signs, on the City Hall Square, were advertising for an office manager. He applied for it and was hired at a salary of twenty dollars per week.

It was at this office, he met Mr. Marvin Stroh when he came in to order some "for rent signs". I met him later when we were window shopping along King Street. He was a tall man, well built, had brown hair, greying at the temples. His voice was gentle as you would expect from such a kindly face. He told us he was a builder by trade and had built most of the houses on Chestnut Street from Mansion to Victoria Streets, and many others in different parts of the City. Since he had twenty-eight on hand, he intended to hold on to them and rent them rather than sell them at a loss.

"How would you people like to rent one?"

"We're sick and tired of apartment living," Clare replied. "What do you think?" he said as he turned and looked at me.

"Good idea. Let's look at some of them."

In order to be within walking distance of Clare's office, we rented 185 Samuel Street from him. It had three rooms downstairs and two bedrooms and a bathroom upstairs The rent was twenty dollars a month, and since I had quit work it would take one week's pay of Clare's to cover that item each month. This is where we lived when our daughter, Fae Maxine, was born.

At eleven-thirty on Christmas morning, 1931, she made her debut into this world at the K-W Hospital. As we bubbled over with happiness about this rare accomplishment, our conversation wandered back to the events of the past four years: the happy moments, our busy schedule, the tough tea biscuits, and the day we first met!

"Yes," said Clare, "remember Lorne coming over to show me a paper and how shocked I was when I looked at it? That was funny! Ya' know, there wasn't a thing written on it!"

One day, when Fae was about two years old, we heard a knock on the door and when I answered it there stood Mr. Stroh with a man and a woman. "These people are interested in buying this house. Could I show them over?"

"Certainly," I answered - (hoping they would hate the place.)

Next day, a 'phone call from him gave us the bad news. The place was sold!

"Don't worry, I have a nice place you can have at 44 Chestnut Street — I'll allow you a month's rent free to help pay your moving expenses!" (The rent there was twenty-five dollars.)

We moved to 44 Chestnut Street and after living there for one year, a knock on the door, the landlord, those familiar words — "Sold this one, but you can have number 28 just down the street, first month's rent free to reimburse you for your trouble!"

Soon after we moved into this one Clare almost blew us to Kingdom Come. The house was too warm, it being the time of the year when you needed a bit of fire, but not too much, and, burning coal in the furnace, it was hard to control. So down the cellar he went to see what he could do to reduce the heat.

Next thing I knew, there was a boom and a commotion underneath me and as I rushed to the cellar door, there stood that sorry looking sight of a husband covered with soot, drenched with water, and with his eyebrows, eyelashes, and half his mustache missing.

"What did you do, sweep the chimney out?"

"No, the furnace exploded when I threw some water on the fire," he said. "Thought I would put it out in a hurry!"

What a mess we had to clean up — soot and water all over the cellar. The house reeked with the acrid fumes of coal gas, smoke and steam, all mixed together. It was sickening!

All the windows were opened - that is, the ones that weren't stuck shut by constant painting - and the doors, to blow out the fumes. While I cleaned up the mess, Clare was in the other room at the stationary tubs stripping off his sooty clothes and washing off the worst of the dirt before he could go upstairs to take a bath.

After the final polish up, he came downstairs looking almost as good as new, a little naked of course, sans eyelashes, eyebrows, and half of his mustache, which he had trimmed very close so that the surviving half could wait for the missing half to catch up to it.

"We can be thankful you didn't injure your eyesight," I said. "Could have been worse! Don't like to be a crepe-hanger, but I wonder what will happen next?"

A few nights later, we were awakened about twelve midnight

by the spasmodic cries of our little girl, Fae. She had often taken these nightmares before and, each time, one of us would slip quietly into her room, pick her up and gently pat her back until she awakened. We had been warned many times that to wake a person out of a nightmare too suddenly could have serious results, so this time, Clare jumped up first, I followed close behind him, and as we raced through her bedroom door, his pyjama string caught on the doorknob and he shot six feet long under her bed with a thunderous thud.

As I stood there in a state of shock, I couldn't seem to make up my mind whether to help my ever-loving husband to his feet or rescue my shrieking baby from her "serious results." This was a decision for Solomon or the Virgilian Dip had my Bible been a bit closer.

As I lifted Fae out of her bed, Clare crawled out from under it, picked himself up, and examined his butt end for bruises.

"Good thing they won't show. With all these bruises and my eyebrows, eyelashes and mustache gone, the fellows at work will be putting me on a billboard to advertise fire prevention week."

The Chestnut Street houses were within walking distance of the Twin City Signs and we were quite contented there, but it seemed to be our fate to keep on moving. This time it was the Sign Company that developed "movitis". Mr. David Hill, owner of Twin City Signs, decided to move the business to a bigger place on Gaukel Street. This was an extra mile for Clare to go to work and since there was no cross-town transportation of any kind, we decided to move closer to their new location.

Chapter V

Eight Times Eight, Times Eight.

When Mr. Stroh learned of our intention, he said, "I would like to keep you people as tenants. I have a house on Herlan Avenue you can have. It's close to your work and to down town. I think you will like it better than the one you're in because it's bigger. I'll give you your first month's rent free again to help with your moving expenses. Take you to see it tonight."

That evening we looked the place over, rented it, and on the First of September, 1934, we moved in. As he predicted, we did like the house much better in every way because it was roomier, had a nice garden with fruit trees, and was handy to downtown.

Since we had cleaned the house thoroughly before we moved in, it didn't take long to get settled and back into our normal routine.

Shortly after supper the next evening, as we sat in the living-room to relax and listen to the radio soap operas, Amos'n Andy and Just Plain Bill, we heard a deafening roar from the region of the dining-room window. We raced over to see what it was, but could see nothing.

"Must have been the wind," Clare said. "Hope that doesn't happen very often. I'll have to look at it in the daylight and tighten it up, I guess."

Back to the chesterfield to hear our stories and, no sooner had we sat down, than it happened again. Clare raced outside just in time to see three boys dart across the road toward the vacant lot and flop down in the grass, where three others were hiding. He rounded them up, held one boy by the arm, and he 'fessed up that it was they who caused the noise on the window by holding a spool against it with the thread stretched across the road into the vacant lot. When they yanked on it it caused the squealing vibration on the window pane. After a stern warning from Clare, and exacting a promise from them that it would not happen again, he released his "prisoner" and the boys went on their way.

By the time we got back in the house, our favourite stories had finished, our relaxation period had come to an abrupt end, and Fae's bedtime peered at us from the kitchen clock.

"Up to bed you go, Bunny," I said to Fae. (A nickname Clare stole from the Amos'n Andy Show when Andy called his girl-friend Honey-Bunny-Boo.)

Fae went up ahead of me and ran into her bedroom and climbed on one of her kindergarten chairs to turn the light on. A flash of light came out of the switch and knocked her flat on the floor. She was slightly stunned, but no serious consequences resulted. A new switch was installed the next day.

Next morning as I went out to throw the old switch into the garbage can my new neighbour came over to bid me the time of the day.

"Good morning," she said. "How do you like your new home?"

"Fine, thank you, we like the location and it's close to Clare's office," I answered as I sniffed the aroma of peach jam escaping from somebody's kitchen.

"Mmmmmm - somebody's making peach jam."

"Yes, I am," she said, "I'll send you a taste of it. It's a new recipe I got this year."

"Thank you, we are very fond of peaches in any way, shape or form. Perhaps, too fond of them. We have been tucking into them so much, Fae has developed a rash. There must be too much acid in them for her."

She looked at me, took a few steps toward her own place, turned back toward me again and said, "Are you — ehhhh — sure — ehhhhh — you know the tenant that moved out — of that house — had bed-bugs? I think she has been bitten by one."

I glared at her, speechless, my stomach turned over, and seemed to divide into four balls of jelly that took up sides to pound at each other like the gloved fists of two prize-fighters! When the fight subsided and I gained enough composure to move my almost paralyzed body, I turned and ran into the house yelling enroute, "I'll call the landlord."

When I got into the house, I raced upstairs into my little girl's room and there on the pink blanket that hung over the foot of her crib was one of those unwanted tenants. I glared at it and it glared at me with all the audacity of an armed intruder.

I rushed to the bathroom, grabbed a handful of toilet tissue, back to the room, snatched the creature up in the paper, squeezed the life out of it, but not hard enough to completely disintegrate the body, so that I could keep the corpus delecti for positive evidence!

Down the stairs I went two at a time and phoned my husband to come home. When he arrived, I opened the paper to show him its contents.

"What's that?"

'I'm not sure, but Mrs. Vogt said the people who moved out had bedbugs! It must be what bit Fae, it wasn't a rash from eating peaches at all!"

"Give it to me. I'll take it down to the Health Department and see for sure," he said as he wheeled around and shot out of the door.

About three-quarters of an hour later, he was back, still

clutching the tissue containing the remains of the pest, and blurted, "That's what it is, all right. Phone the landlord quick."

Phone the landlord I did and when he answered, I said "What kind of people did you have in this house? It's infested."

"No!" he gasped. "I'll be right over."

When he arrived, we showed him the evidence. He apologized for getting us into such a mess and then went over to the telephone to arrange for a fumigation.

"Sleep with the lights on tonight and I will be here in the morning with the exterminators. Nothing will happen if you leave the lights on."

We did as he advised and first thing in the morning, the men came and took over the house.

"You people will have to stay out of here for three days and you must take out your silverware and scissors. We are using hydracyanic acid and it will ruin them. It sure does a job on the bugs too. You know, these things can lie dormant for twenty years behind wall paper and then come out. That's why we use this acid. It's a sure thing."

We watched as they placed a ten gallon crock on the floor of each room, sealed the window frames and doors with masking tape, hung their gas masks around their necks so that they could don them when they ignited the acid in the crocks, and then we left.

"Believe me, I'm moving out of here when this is over," I told them.

"Oh, no, don't do that — you will be safe here when this is done. If you move, you could get into them again, or you could pick them up on a moving truck. The movers are supposed to sweep their trucks out carefully, but they don't always do it. Better stay where you are. All you need is one. They increase so fast. You know there is no male and female to these bugs. Every bug lays eggs, eight at a time. They hatch and lay eight more and so on."

As I listened to him I thought - eight times eight is sixty-four, times eight is five hundred and twelve — and the three of us scurried out of the front door. As we crossed the lawn, we could see two big signs, one at the side of the house, the other at the front: "Danger - Keep Out."

For three days Fae and I stayed with my sister Margaret in Preston and Clare stayed at the Mayfair Hotel so that he could look after his job. When we returned to the house, silverware and scissors in hand, we found the windows and doors wide open to let the acid fumes escape, and one of the fumigators was just removing the danger signs.

As we entered, I noticed the tattered strips of masking tape hanging like stalactites from every window and door frame in the house. What a mess to greet us just a few days after we had cleaned the place so thoroughly before moving in.

We ripped the tattered fragments of tape from the windows and doors, cleaned the window panes, waxed the woodwork and floors, and, two days later, no one could have guessed what that house had gone through, unless, of course, they put their nose too close to the woodwork, and got a whiff of that nauseating acid the fumigators used.

In the kitchen and bathroom, where we washed the walls and woodwork, the odor was intensified by the use of water, so we decided to paint those rooms. We didn't particularly care for the colors the landlord had on them anyway.

"We will paint them ourselves," Clare said. "We can't very well ask Mr. Stroh to do it when he gave us the first month's rent free and then ran into this fumigating job. After all, that wasn't his fault either."

A few days later, when the painting was completed, we sat down with our daughter to enjoy an hour of relaxation before bedtime. "The peach season will soon be over," said Clare. "You can feel a bit of a chill in the air."

The next day after Clare went to work, Fae was settled in bed for her afternoon nap and, since the air seemed even chillier, I decided to build a fire in the furnace. I put in several newspapers, some small sticks of wood, ignited it, closed the furnace door, and proceeded upstairs to the living-room to have a rest. I turned the radio on to listen to the Ma Perkins' show, stretched my weary self out on the chesterfield, and as she was instructing her son, Willie, to hold the fort for her while she went to lunch, the smell of smoke struck my nostrils! Smoke was pouring from every register in the house!

I jumped to my feet, bolted upstairs, grabbed my three-year old daughter, carried her downstairs, out the back door, over to my neighbours, and yelled, "My house is on fire!"

Mr. Vogt rushed over, went in the back door and straight to

the cellar. He reached his hand into the damper on the smoke pipe and pulled out yards and yards of crumpled newspaper.

"It happens every time," he said. "I'm a fireman for the City of Kitchener. Good thing I was off duty. Every time they fumigate a house, they plug this pipe and forget to take it out. How are the people to know if they don't tell them?"

"Must get ready to go to work," he continued, as he opened the windows and doors to let the smoke escape.

"Thanks a million - sure am glad you were home - we've really had the course since we moved in here," I lamented, as he slipped out of the back door and across the lawn to his home.

Chapter VI

Have An Eye For Bunty.

Moving, unwanted tenants, the stench of hydracyanic acid still emanating from the woodwork, lungs full of smoke, time for a change of scenery! "We'll go up to the farm for the weekend," I said. Clare agreed, and Fae danced around the room twittering to her doll about Uncle Frank's lambs, kittens, dog, and Bunty, the ram.

We caught the early train on Saturday and Frank met us at the Paisley Station with the old Star car to drive us to the farm. Dinner was ready when we arrived, and as we tucked into home-made pork sausage, mashed potatoes, buttered carrots, cabbage salad, apple pie, maple syrup, tea biscuits, nine-day pickles, washed down with several cups of tea, Frank drawled, "Remember that quart jar of pickles you brought up last time you were here, Florence? Well, I took it to the Fair and got first prize in the Sour Pickle Class."

"Sour pickles, indeed! Those were made from a tested recipe I took out of Good Housekeeping Magazine. They were **sweet** pickles and I did'nt forget the sugar because we ate plenty of the same batch ourselves."

"Well, anyway, they weren't marked, so I entered them in the Sour Pickle Class and got first prize!" he repeated with a half-grin and a shrug of his shoulders.

Mother blurted, "Let's get at the dishes. Uncle Frank Pearce is coming over with his harp this evening. We'll have some music."

Uncle Frank arrived before we finished the dishes and the men took their places in the living-room. Uncle Frank had his harp, Dad, his violin, Brother Frank, his banjo, and Clare was at the piano. The strains of the Sailor's Horn Pipe, the pounding of feet, keeping time on the floor, mingled with the percussion sounds from the kitchen crockery, presented an ear-splitting din that shouldn't happen to anybody!

When the musicians got down to "When Father Papered the Parlour", "Turkey in the Straw", or "When You and I were Young Maggie," it was a sure sign that they were running out of tunes and bedtime was close at hand.

On the way upstairs, Frank told us that he got a bit bruised up earlier that day. "I was bending over to tie my shoelace and that crazy ram came up behind me and sent me flying," he said.

Next morning, after breakfast, Fae and I went outside and climbed the orchard fence to pick some applies. The orchard was on the side of a steep hill, and we could see Frank at the top of it looking over his sheep. Bunty, the ram, had edged to within ten feet of him, and as I turned toward the apple tree, Frank shouted, "Have an eye for the ram!"

I screamed at Fae, "Jump over the fence," and she made it, but the old fence leaned over with my weight and I hung there straddling it like a giant clothes pin. As I struggled to make the fence wire lean the other way, I suddenly found myself in an upside down position gazing up hill at Bunty still standing like something cut out of stone, glaring at his guffawing master!

With Fae's help, I dislodged myself, stood up and shouted, "I'll get back on you for this. I thought he was after us for sure!"

Fae rushed to the house ahead of me to tell the folks what had happened, and when I got to the door, I heard a burst of laughter, and Mother saying, "I saw the whole performance out of the dining-room window. I wondered what the hurry was!"

"First he puts my sweet pickles in the sour pickle class and then he scares us to death with that ram!" I shouted. "Guess we'll get ready to go back to Kitchener — this weekend change of scenery will be the death of me!"

Chapter VII

September Comes Again.

It was 1935 and all year long business had been falling off. Each pay day, Mr. Hill asked Clare if he could possibly get another position. "Don't want to lay you off — but things are bad — you can see that by the books — can't hang on to you much longer. I'll have to take a girl on in your place at less money."

The blow came in September. "Sorry - can't afford to keep you any longer."

Every morning, for six weeks, Clare donned his well-worn shoes and pounded the pavements for the third time since the depression started. Every evening he came in tired and disgusted. "This looking for a job is worse than any day's work I've ever done. Why, they just laugh in your face. Did you look to see if there is anything in the paper today?"

"No, I didn't - not much use looking there," I said, as I opened the paper just to please him.

And there it was — a boxed advertisement — "The City of Kitchener wants a clerk in the Tax Department," I yelled.

"Have to have plenty of pull to get in there," he said. "There will be dozens after it. But if it's pull I need, it's pull I'll get."

With that, he went to the telephone and set to work gathering up his "pull". Within three days, he had recommendations from his last employer Mr. David Hill, their auditor Mr. Ralph Brock, Mr. Albert Dunker, owner of the largest contracting firm in Kitchener, and my former employer Mr. W. P. Clement. He sent in his application with these recommendations attached, and three days later was informed that the forty-two applications had been weeded down to four, and that they would like him to come in the next day to "try out" for the job.

Each one was tested on typing and cash counting. Two more were weeded out, and the contest was between Clare and one other man. Typing went fine for both of them, but when it came to counting cash, Clare's eight years' experience in the Bank of Montreal, gave him the edge for both speed and accuracy. He got the position and commenced work on October 15th, 1935, at a salary of one hundred dollars per month.

Chapter VIII

The Jiggily John.

A job in the City Hall at a hundred a month! Our house troubles over! Security at last!

As we discussed our good fortune, I turned toward the window and noticed our landlord Mr. Stroh and a young couple get out of his car. They proceeded toward the front door and knocked. I answered, Mr. Stroh introduced the people, and said, "These people would like to look over this house. They want to buy one in this vicinity."

I invited them in, they looked the house over and the next day we were informed that they had purchased it and we would have to move.

"Don't worry, though, you can have the one at 33 Chestnut and I will give you the first month's rent free just as I did before."

On the first of November we moved into this bigger, almost new house, with the first month's rent free. It was built on the side of a huge hill that is bounded by Lancaster, Luella, Victoria and Chestnut streets, and just half a block from the Canadian National railroad tracks.

The movers placed the heavier furniture in its proper rooms, the electrician, who lived across the street, came to connect up the stove so that we could prepare supper. After supper we went upstairs to set up the beds, Fae's first and then ours. Clare went into the bathroom and I stayed in Fae's bedroom to put the sheets and blankets on. Suddenly, the house started to shimmy! I heard a voice from the bathroom shouting, "What the devil's wrong with this toilet? I wonder if it always shakes this way? This place has got a jiggily John."

"Maybe it's the train going by. Surely, we don't have to put up with that every time a train goes by," I answered back.

Sleep came slowly that night. There was no more shimmying but I had the feeling he was thinking the same thing I was. Now, what have we got into? Probably it WAS the train going by. We'll take notice tomorrow.

The next day, I heard several trains go by. How could I help it with a whistle as shrill as they had? Enough to wake the dead, to be sure, but it didn't jiggle the house. Later in the day, when Clare came in from work, I knew by the silly grin on his face, that he must have solved the mystery of "the jiggily John."

"That's not the only thing that jiggled," he said. "There was an earthquake last night! When I told the fellas about our "jiggily John", they went into conniptions, and one of them said all their dishes flew out of the cupboard. Seems it was worse in some parts of the city than in others!"

"Guess this house is sitting on rock. I thought it was going to slide down off the hill last night when it started to shimmy!" What a thought! I wonder if it would slide down! Oh, well, if it does, there's a dozen others that will go with it, and anyway it would have to be a bigger earthquake than that to send them tumbling! They're well-built houses too, Mr. Stroh always builds a good house. He builds each one as if he had to live in it himself for the rest of his life. We'll start unpacking the rest of the boxes tomorrow and get things straightened around. "We should be very comfortable here." I quavered.

Next morning, at breakfast, I noticed that Fae didn't look too good - rather tired - she was restless during the night too. I heard her twisting, turning, and banging her hand against the wall. After Clare went to work, I went outside to shake a mat and my new neighbour Mrs. Exton came over to talk to me.

"Lots to do when you first move in," she remarked. "How do you like your place?"

"I like it fine - rather frightened the other night though when that earthquake shook it. We didn't know what in the world was wrong with the place, jiggling like that. Fae hasn't slept too well since we moved in either. Guess she isn't quite used to the place yet."

"Same with the other peoples' children. They had three little ones and they used to cry and cry when they put them to bed. You know the people that just moved out" — she hesitated — raised her eyebrows and shook her head.

"Don't tell me — let me tell you — the people that just moved out — had - - - - - - - - - "

When I choked awake, my nose lodged in a bottle of smelling salts, I felt the November grass chilling my prostrate form and a mad river rushing through my brain roaring, "Every bug lays eggs, eight at a time; eight times eight, times eight, sticky paper around the windows and doors, hydracyanic, hydracyanic, hydracyanic acid, take out your silver and scissors, your silver and scissors, three days in a hotel, three days, three days, three days — don't move — you're safer here! Call the landlord!"

"Oh, dear, not this one too! Why don't they tell me instead of moving out. They will take them to another place. I'm so sorry to get you into this again. We'll fumigate right away."

Here we go again! Arrangements for three days in a hotel. Crocks of burning hydracyanic acid in the middle of each room, windows and doors sealed with sticky paper, furnace pipe stuffed with wads of paper, men running around with gas masks on, and that infernal sign out front "DANGER KEEP OUT". People must have wondered if we had gone berserk and were holding them at bay.

Houses sold over our heads, earthquakes, jiggily Johns, unwanted tenants — who wouldn't go berserk? But things quieted down after the fumigation and we had the house shipshape for a white Christmas.

There was a lot of snow that winter. There were many children on the street, too, for Fae to play with. Often we had two dozen of them playing in our driveway. The Zettels had eight and so did the Kelly's and several families numbered half that many. There was a good sleigh riding hill in the lot next door running down from that cliff behind our house.

That cliff didn't look so bad in the winter when it was covered with snow, all white and clean looking, but in the summer it jarred me to no end. I always felt as if I would like to reach out and shove it away so that I could see right down Queen Street. What a view it would have made in the daytime, all those beautiful houses with big trees around the front and light standards with huge white globes diffusing their brilliance through the foliage in the evening! Well, we couldn't move the hill, but we didn't have to worry about that very long.

It was in the spring, toward the end of March, I looked out of the kitchen window and saw three people hovering around the back, looking first at the house and then at the sudden incline. I could tell by their smiles and the motions they made with their hands that they figured something nice could be done with that hill.

I went outside to see if they were figuring on moving it so that I would have a better view, when I realized it was Mr. Stroh. He introduced me to the couple with him.

"I would like you to meet Mrs. Rolands and Mr. Rolands, who have the flower shop down town. They would like to buy this house. Could I show them inside?"

They went through the house, and then went on their way. Next day, a call from the landlord. "They bought the house and I'm afraid I haven't another one to give you this time. Sorry, too, you've been with me for ten years. Nothing vacant at the moment."

"Well, at least this is a switch. We have five weeks to find ourselves a new landlord," Clare groaned.

"Wish we had a down payment so that we could buy a house," I replied.

"No use wishing things like that, we'll have to take an apartment for a while, save some money, and then buy one," was his comforting answer. And this is exactly what we did.

Chapter IX

My Most Embarrassing Moment.

We found an apartment at 18 Pequegnat Avenue. Five rooms on the second floor of an old, but well-kept house. It was the old Shanks' home. Sort of a spooky place in a way with its huge entrance hall, solid sliding doors between the hall and livingroom that were kept locked because of the two tenants living in the house, a heavy door leading into the dining-room and another closing off the cellar steps. The stairs leading up to our apartment twisted twice into landings and led into a hall that ran the full length of the house from front to back, and then turned to the left to reveal a back stairway sneaking up from the kitchen below to afford the tenant downstairs a direct route to the bathroom which we shared. Our rooms flanked the long hall, three on one side and two on the other. The extra door on that side led up to a scary attic. But still it was a handy place at times. We put an extra bed up there to accommodate our overflow of overnight guests or, on occasion, to help the people downstairs with theirs.

We paid our rent to the tenant downstairs and they in turn paid the rent for the whole house to the Bender Realty Company. Then when they moved out a few months later and a new tenant moved in, we took over and paid the rent to Bender's. We took it for granted that Benders owned the place.

It was a busy morning as usual - meals to get, dishes to wash - floors to clean - question and answer period with five year old daughter - telephone ringing - doors to answer - battered knees to bandage - dinner to prepare for that tired and hungry husband.

Dinner hour is over - more dishes - more telephone calls - more door knocking - getting daughter ready for afternoon session in Kindergarten.

Away she goes, hippity-hop, laughing and waving "Bye-bye Mummy". "Come straight home from school, Honey". To our upper duplex I retreated, forgetting to lock the door.

Peace, perfect peace, for a couple of hours! Did that chesterfield ever look so inviting? Down full length my ninety pounds collapsed on it - soft music wafting from the radio. A state of semi-consciousness soon came over me.

The front screen door rattled - I heard it open! Footsteps in the downstairs hall! I leaped to my feet and down to the first landing two steps at a time. There he was - teetering precariously from side to side. He's drunk, I thought!

I lunged down the rest of the steps to the hallway yelling, "Who are you, who are you?" I grabbed his coat lapels, pushed him backwards out the door, threw him across the wide verandah, stepped back into the hall and locked the screen door.

As soon as he regained his composure, he said, "I'm so sorry, Mrs. Hammond, It's all my fault, you have never met me before - I am your landlord, Allan Haist, and I should have knocked instead of walking in."

He went on to explain that he wanted to get some pipes from the cellar to use at another property he owned. As the eviction notice, the for rent sign and my furniture neatly piled in the moving truck loomed up in front of me - I unlocked the door and permitted him to re-enter and proceed with his business.

I learned later from a friend that this victim of my fright had had Polio when he was a child and that accounted for his peculiar locomotion. Was I embarrassed? That is the understatement of the century.

As I sat on the steps to unravel my twisted thoughts and quiet my thumping heart, I could hear the clang of pipes as he pulled them from between the joists and made his way up the stairs toward the front hall where I was sitting. I held the door open for him, apologized for throwing him out, and away he teetered down Pequegnat Avenue toward the house he was repairing, one end of the long water pipes braced under his arm, the other end dragging on the sidewalk behind him.

Later in the evening, during that quiet interlude when children are tucked in their beds, the day's events in father's office and the home come to the fore, and this evening was no exception.

"Quiet day at the office today for a change," he said. "Something bothering you?"

"Yes, I met our landlord today - Benders don't own this place. Allan Haist does."

"Well, that's nothing to worry about is it?"

"No, it's nothing to worry about, except that I didn't know him and when he walked in the front hall I threw him out the door and half way across that big verandah. I thought he was a drunk the way he wobbled across the hall toward the cellar door."

When Clare finally extricated himself from his knots of laughter, he said, "Perhaps this would be a good time to buy a place of our own."

"There's two hundred in the bank we can use, and we can borrow some from the Finance Company and - and - . Well, let's go to see Mr. Stroh. I always liked living in 28 Chestnut - perhaps he will sell that one to us."

We saw him the next evening and purchased the place from him for thirty-three hundred dollars, with a down payment made up of our two hundred, one hundred and forty from the Finance Company, Mr. Stroh accepted our promissory note for one hundred and sixty dollars, and we assumed the mortgage already on the property to Mr. Urias Weber of twenty-eight hundred dollars.

So then we were the proud possessors of our own home and three mortgages.

Twenty dollars a month to the finance company (they charged twenty-five per cent. interest) and ten dollars a month to Mr. Stroh reduced the membership of our mortgage alliance to one - Mr. Urias Weber.

We thought it would be clear sailing from this time on. Anything was better than living in that other place with all its halls and sneaky stairways. There was even a stairway from the kitchen down to the cellar that I didn't know about for a long time. I learned about that one day when I was in the cellar doing my laundry and the lady on the main floor almost scared me to death when she opened her kitchen door and shouted down that my telephone was ringing!

Another time I couldn't easily forget was the day that Fae ran down the hall to go to the bathroom and her screams echoed through the flat as she raced back toward the living-room, where I was dusting, looking as if she had seen a ghost, and how I took her hand and led her back to see what had frightened her. I almost screamed myself as I saw the toilet draped in billows of black silk, the only sign that a human being lurked inside was evidenced by the wizened features peering out of the folds.

Then a voice from below the back stairway assured us, "It's only my Grandma. She should have shut the bathrooom door. She's ninety-five years old. Can't think so well anymore. Sorry she frightened you."

And how could we forget that busy day when Fae played quietly in her bedroom and, as I slipped down the hall to see if everything was okay, I met her coming out the door, scissors in hand, and with one side of her hair cropped above her ear? What could Daddy do but cut the other side off to balance the situation. These unpleasant memories did give way, however, to the more pleasant thoughts of our new surroundings.

Our new home with its many windows was bright and cheerful as the sunbeams danced happily through the placc. It even made us forget, for a time, that we were bogged down by the depression. We didn't mind sleeping in sugar bag nighties, on sugar bag sheets and pillow cases, or drying our dishes on sugar bag tea towels. We didn't mind wearing house dresses made from flour bags, even if Robin Hood did refuse to surrender to the bleach pot. His presence with his bow and arrow gave a colorful finish to the dress, and saved us the time and expense of decorating it Economies like this were necessary to eke out a living or to help replace a worn out appliance on which the last instalment still had to be paid.

Finance Companies, with their twenty-five per cent. interest rate, were the only ones that really ENJOYED the depression. People who inherited a sizeable estate from their parents or a rich uncle didn't fare too badly either, but the average family wouldn't have had the bare necessities of life had it not been for the instalment plan.

All the words in the world could not explain the situation half as well as a cartoon carried by the Kitchener Daily Record on January 10, 1936 . . . .

KITCHENER DAILY RECORD, FRIDAY, JANUARY 10, 1936.

If the things that are paid for were the only ones visible!
—Der Lustige Sachse, Leipzig.

How well I remember the holiday I spent at the farm with Fae, which prompted me to write this letter to Clare who had stayed at home to do some work around the garden:

R.R. 2,
Dobbinton, Ont., July 15/36.

Dear Clare:

Oh, what a beautiful day! When I woke up this morning the sun was shining and balmy breezes were blowing in the window!

Grandpa went to town to take the cream in and to get groceries. When he got home Grandma found he was five dollars short in his change. She phoned the store but the clerk said their cash balanced that day.

Grandma was furious! She slammed the door as she flounced out to gather the eggs so Grandpa decided to wash the dishes. Just as he was throwing the greasy dishwater out the door, Grandma came around the corner with her basket of eggs and she got the pan of water in her face! I thought there would be a battle royal but instead Grandma looked down at her dripping clothes and burst out laughing. So did the rest of us.

Later in the afternoon Grandpa went out to the barn to repair the side where some of the boards had blown off during that last storm. We could hear him hammering away for a while and then everything was quiet. Frank looked out the back door and all he could see was Grandpa's head sticking out of the barn! He had nailed on one board too many and couldn't get back in.

Frank yelled for Grandma and me. "Look up there! If his feet slip off the ledge, he could hang himself!"

"For two pins I'd leave him there." Grandma puffed, as we dashed for the barn.

Never a dull moment around here! Good place for a holiday! See you at the week end.

Love,

Flo. and Fae.

Chapter X

1939-45 War Years.

The country was still nursing its bruises from the depression when, on September 3rd, 1939, the second world war broke out.

Women enlisted in the various auxiliary services so that the men in the Army, Navy, and Airforce were available for the more difficult posts and actual fighting. Canada, like other countries, emerged from its unemployment problem into the shortage of help problem for the "home front". The Government demanded that everyone do his or her part. Married women worked while their children were in school or the smaller ones were in day-care centres.

For the first time in history, the Kitchener Public Utilities Commission hired women as street-car conductors. I was called back to work at Clement's Law Office where Mr. W. P. Clement was holding the nucleus of the business together until the enlisted members of the firm returned from the war if, indeed, they would be lucky enough to return.

It was in 1941 when we sold our home on Chestnut Street and purchased 74 Doehn Street. (The German spelling of this name so confused people, that the residents on the street persuaded the City Officials to change it to the phonetic way - "Dane".)

Shortage of materials soon became apparent which caused us to improvise in many places. Since the material was needed for parachutes, silk or nylon hose vanished from the stores and then the trend was to go barelegged. The office bosses co-operated in this patriotic gesture and gave us permission to go to work sans hosiery.

Fully automatic ovens were unknown at that time and as we had the "turn the top off, and the bottom on low" variety, which we couldn't leave too many hours because we had to conserve electricity, we cooked our scalloped or baked potatoes on the ledge inside the door of the coal furnace. This worked well unless a high wind made the fire burn up, and so would the potatoes!

Food shortages made it necessary for the Government to institute rationing. Coupons were issued for meat, butter, sugar, tea, soap, and gasoline, and since we couldn't buy tires for our car because it wasn't essential to the war effort, we sold it to the owner of a flour mill.

Sometimes we secured some extra butter when Mrs. Mausberg, our good Jewish neighbour, would give us an extra coupon or two, since their Kosher cooking did not allow them to use their full allotment. And, once in a while, we saved the cream off the top of the milk and when we had enough to half fill a large jar, we would tie the jar to the gyrator of the washing machine and churn some extra butter.

To eke out extra soap for the family wash, the whole family used to save every drop or scrap of fat so that Arthur Jefkins, my brother-in-law, could make soap out of it the way he remembered his mother doing when they lived on the farm in Doon. Then the spoils were shared pro rata.

Short skirts were in style during this era and since men's trousers were wide in the legs, if a lady friend had a new skirt on, it was a common occurrence to hear her say, "I made it out of a pair of Jim's trousers. They were awfully shiny at the seat, so I turned the material and made myself a skirt."

Although our lives were a series of improvisations and hard work, we had no complaints. All one had to do was to read the newspapers or listen to the news on the radio about the suffering of our soldiers and relatives on the other side of the ocean and we considered ourselves very fortunate. We wondered sometimes if we would live to see the end of the war.

Our weekly schedule had been something like this — Monday to Friday - up at six o'clock - make breakfast - wash dishes - stick potatoes inside the furnace door while still chewing last bites. Then a wild dash down Dane Street to catch "Leaping Lena", Kitchener's bucking trolley. I seldom missed it, but sat there wondering if I would retain my breakfast till I arrived at Frederick Street. Arrived at the office in nick of time. An hour-and-a-half for lunch (Clare had an hour-and-a quarter). Rushed home for dinner because Fae was only ten years old, and it broke the day for her when she came from school. Swallowed dinner - washed dishes - saw Fae off for the afternoon session - back down Dane Street - almost with a head-on collision with the trolley! Made the one-thirty deadline at the office. Worked until five o'clock. Fae prepared supper (bless her).

Clare and Fae washed the dishes while I went to the basement to do the family washing in the old-fashioned wringer-type washer. Bed at twelve-midnight. Tuesday evening I did the ironing. Bed at midnight. Wednesday evening - mending - worked up extra butter gyrated in the washing machine. Bed at midnight. Thursday evening - cleaned the upstairs. Bed at midnight. Friday evening - cleaned the downstairs. Bed at midnight. Saturday - worked at the office in the morning. Home about one o'clock. In the afternoon - shopped for week's supply of groceries or clothes for the family. Sunday - Church in the morning - short drive in the country to visit family member. Occasionally, trip to farm near Paisley to visit Clare's people.

In our summer holidays, we took one week at the beach, the other to paint the house!

(Oh, my gosh, I'm exhausted just thinking about it!)

The hard work did finally catch up with us! Clare was worn to a frazzle and I had to discontinue my work in Clement's Office. How well I remember the last day I worked! When I got off old "Leaping Lena" at the foot of Dane Street, the slight upgrade to my home seemed like a mountain!

Chapter XI

Shenanigans in the Mortuary.

I was just getting used to leading a normal homelife, when one day, as I sauntered along King Street on a window shopping tour, I met Mr. Goldring, the manager of the Royal Typewriter Company.

"You're just the person I want to see," he said. "I just came from the Bradshaw Funeral Home and Mr. Bradshaw is in dire need of a secretary. Would you consider taking the position?"

In spite of my protests, his argument that "a change is as good as a rest" prevailed, and I consented to try it for a while.

The secretary's duties there consisted of taking down the whole funeral service in shorthand to make up a booklet for the bereaved family. The booklet also recorded the list of donors of flowers or cash donations for charities.

It was interesting work and as Mr. Goldring assured me, it was a change! The first three days went very well. I was catching on to the routine. Then the fourth day was one of those beautiful, too-nice-to-go-to-work days. The bus I was on was the early one. I reached up, pulled the cord, and the bus stopped one block from my destination. When I alighted and sauntered toward the office, the building looked like a castle as the sun danced on its new coat of white paint.

I entered the door, put my purse in the desk drawer and went into the next room. A woman lay there. She was dead. Across the hall was another room. I entered it. Another dead woman was lying at the far end. To the right was a third room. I did not enter. I just peered in at the door. A corpse was lying there - a man. They had been there since I had left at five o'clock yesterday.

I returned to my desk. The sound of voices came from the back hall. No sound of footsteps; the floor was carpeted. Four men appeared in the doorway. They were Mr. Bradshaw, the Manager; Harry, the senior mortician; Bob and Dennis, assistant morticians.

"Good morning, Mr. Bradshaw," I said. "Good morning, Mrs. Hammond. I will be down at the Smith home on Queen Street, South. If anything comes up, you can reach me there," he instructed me as he hurried out of the front door. Harry turned to me and said, "We will be in the back office." He motioned the other men to follow him.

There was work to be done. A funeral service to be typed for the Glebe family, donors of flowers to be listed, thank you cards to be sent to the sympathizers, cash donations to be acknowledged, letters to write, and a phone to be answered.

The phone rang - I answered it - "Bradshaw's Funeral Home." A familiar voice said, "Mrs. Hammond, I am still down at Smith's place on Queen Street, South. Have the boys bring the hearse down, Mrs. Smith died." "Yes, Mr. Bradshaw, it will be down immediately."

I buzzed Harry's office. Harry answered. "Mr. Bradshaw wants you to send the hearse to 222 Queen Street, South, Mrs. Smith has died," I told him. "O.K.," answered Harry.

I resumed my typing. A shadow attracted my eyes to the window. It was the hearse backing out. Away it went. Half an hour later, I saw it return.

The phone rang - I answered - "Bradshaw's Funeral Home."

"This is Bob, Mrs. Hammond. Are YOU ever in trouble - you sent the hearse to Mrs. Smith's place and she isn't dead. The old man is seething. He's still down there trying to make it right with the family." Then Bob hung up.

My chin dropped. I felt the blood leaving my face. My stomach went into knots. I just can't faint! My fingers would not move over the typewriter keys. My brain swirled with thoughts - what will I do - don't care if I get fired - don't like being on call seven days a week anyway - but this is my girl friend's grandmother. What will they think of me? How can I face them?

Again - the shadows - a car came into the driveway. It was Mr. Bradshaw's car.

Three faces peeked around by office door - one above the other. They were giggling - Harry, Bob, and Dennis. "It's O.K., Mrs. Hammond," Bob said. "We were just kidding, Mrs. Smith is dead, the body is here. You are now initiated into the Royal Order of the Rigor Mortis Club. Oh, oh, the boss is coming," he gasped, as they made their escape down the back hall.

Six weeks was the extent of my experience as secretary to a mortician. Being on call seven days a week was too much for my limited strength and my obligation to my home and family.

Chapter XII

Exit - "Leaping Lena"

The war ended in 1945 and immediately the country turned to making the much needed civilian supplies. The Wartime Prices & Trade Board had kept a keen eye on prices during and after the war until the supply could make its own adjustment.

Before long automatic washing machines appeared on the market. Stoves with ovens so automatic you could set them to turn on, cook the dinner and turn off again while you were out playing bridge.

In 1947, the Public Utilities Commissioners decided that Kitchener's street-cars had to go. They were replaced by electric trolley buses at a cost of twenty thousand dollars each. We were glad to get rid of "Leaping Lena" and have those nice new buses, but the cost was greater than any one of us expected. The day of their first run was the saddest day of our lives since Carol Schmidt, our seven year old neighbour, was almost instantly killed by one of them as she tried to board it on her way to Sunday School.

The story, as it was told to us, was that she had been the last one in line and as the woman ahead of her got on the bus the driver could not see Carol and he closed the door which caused her to slip down the snow bank under the wheels of the bus. Some men on a Hydro truck saw her, rushed her to Dr. McTaggart's Office three or four blocks away where she died.

Rationing of gasoline and tires ended which made it possible for us to run a car for pleasure.

Trips to the farm in a space of two hours did away with those five hour train rides we experienced during the war, with long waits at Guelph and Palmerston. Things had changed somewhat in the interim, since my Mother had died in January, 1939, Clare's Mother died in September that same year, and Grandpa Hammond and Frank batched it on the farm for a short time. Then Frank married Ruby Caldwell, who came there to live, which gave the farm that much needed woman's touch to aid in its successful operation.

A sense of humour is one of Ruby's greatest attributes; if we saw her face light up into a grin from ear to ear, we always knew something had happened the previous week and that she was about to relate the incident to us, for example, the time that Frank came in from the barn to get some money from his Dad to go to town to buy chop for the cattle.

Frank hurried in from the barn and told Dad he had to have some money. Dad went upstairs to get some and as he came down with a two dollar bill in his hand he noticed some manure on the stairs that had fallen off his shoe. He picked it up and went to the kitchen with the manure in one hand and the two dollar bill in the other. As he lifted the stove lid, he threw the two dollar bill into the flames and handed the manure to Frank.

"What am I supposed to do with this?" Frank asked, as he gazed into Dad's wide-open mouth.

"Oh, my gosh, that's all the money we've got!" Dad exclaimed.

Chapter XIII

The Stampede.

It was in September, 1950, that Fae, Audrey Hertzberger, Margaret Richardson, Janet Ziegler, and Pat Bailey went to Port Elgin to spend the Labor Day weekend with Pat Bailey's parents at their cottage. Except for a few short trips in the immediate vicinity, Clare and I took advantage of the beautiful weekend to do some work around home. We got up early that Monday morning so that Clare could rid the lawn of the fresh crops of weeds the rain had brought up, and I always liked to get an early start with the laundry. Just as I was running a sheet through the wringer, the telephone rang. I pulled and tugged at the sheet to speed it up, flopped it in the basket and raced up the stairs.

"Is this Mrs. Hammond?" the voice at the other end said.

"Yes," I answered.

"This is Dr. Nelles of Port Elgin speaking," he went on.

"Your daughter Fae has had an accident. We have her in the hospital at Southampton. I wanted to phone you last night, but she wouldn't let me. She made me promise not to phone you until this morning. She was thrown from a horse!"

"How bad is it?"

"She'll be all right, but she'll have to stay in the hospital here for a while. You will find her breathing very raspy. She has a Plural Rub. (An injury to the lining of the lung, he explained later.)

"I'll be right up. Tell Fae I'm on my way." I said.

Since Clare and I decided that I should stay close to the hospital until Fae could be brought to Kitchener, he stayed at home. I drove eighty miles an hour and my first stop was the Doctor's office in Port Elgin. After chastising me for driving so fast, he went on to explain the extent of Fae's injuries.

"Quite a gash all down one side, there's a Plural Rub, the second rib from the collarbone is disconnected from the breast-bone, and the cartilages here (pointing to his floating rib) are twisted like a dishcloth. They will never change. Cartilages do not heal, but the other things will right themselves in time. The shock is a bad thing. It will probabily take three years for her to get over that."

I thanked him for his kindness and left for the Southampton Hospital. When I arrived the first thing Fae said was, "I made the doctor promise not to phone you until this morning. I wanted you to get your night's sleep. You couldn't do anything for me anyway. I just screamed when they poured alcohol all over my injury."

After spending an hour with Fae I drove back to Paisley where Clare's Aunt Mary lived to see if she would let me stay at her place while Fae had to remain in the hospital. She said she was glad to have me and when I told her about the accident, she gasped, "I saw that mixup with the horses! Uncle Frank and I were driving by the Riding Ranch and I said to Frank, 'There must be something wrong the way the horses are running all over the place!' Oh, I didn't know Fae was in it or we would have stayed to help look after her."

Aunt Mary's home was five miles from the hospital which made it possible for me to visit Fae twice a day. As I arrived at the hospital the day after the accident, I met Mrs. Bailey in the corridor. She told me she had stayed in the hospital all night with Fae and Audrey. Audrey was released that day. Bit by bit, during my visits, the story unravelled itself.

It seems that the girls thought they would finish their weekend holiday by going horseback riding. Fae did'nt feel too well that morning when she got up and she didn't want to go, but Pat coaxed and coaxed so that she finally gave in and away they went. They waited for some time for the attendants and the former bunch of young people to return with the horses. There were people of all ages milling around to watch the sport. A few two and three-year-olds hung close to their mothers or sisters. The attendants prepared Fae's bunch for their ride and helped them mount. Then, just as the attendants mounted, a horse bolted from behind the barn dragging a large roll of old fence wire, charged toward them, and as it flew by, each horse in turn was struck by the wire which caused them to take off in every direction. The horse which was dragging the wire ended up on the beach several blocks away. The onlookers ran for cover, one two-year old was thrown over the fence by her ten-year-old sister, and then she hopped over herself.

Margaret Richardson slid off the hind-end of her horse as it jumped over a four foot fence a few feet from where they had been standing. She was shaken up but was not seriously hurt. Pat Bailey's horse dashed out of the L-shaped lane to the street, jumped over the hood of a Ford car, tearing off a strip of chrome, and continued on until it reached the main street of Port Elgin five blocks away, Pat still hanging on for dear life. Audrey Hertzberger managed to stay on her horse until the one Margaret Richardson slid from collided with it which caused the two of them to fall back to back in the middle of the road about half a block from the Ranch. When the rescuers got there, Audrey was on the ground between the two horses, unconscious. Her shoe was found a short distance away. Fae, all this time, was lying by the lane fence, badly injured, where she was thrown as her horse shot around the sharp turn in the lane. Since some of the frightened horses started to gallop back into the lane, she thought she would be trampled for sure, but someone heard her cries and came to her aid. The ambulance was called to take her and Audrey to the hospital. Audrey was released the next morning, but Fae remained for a week, when Dr. Nelles allowed us to have her transferred to Kitchener by ambulance. I reached home a few hours before the ambulance.

Although I had kept in touch with Clare by phone during that awful week, he was fit to be tied with concern about Fae. He told us he thought we might be covering up her condition to some degree so that he would be able to carry on his arduous duties in the Tax Office and in our home. He also told us that as soon as the news of the accident had appeared in the local newspaper, he had been beseiged with calls all week long until he finally had to take the receiver off the hook in order to eat a meal.

When Fae was transferred from the stretcher to her bed by the Ambulance driver and his assistant, we filled in some of the loose ends of the story for Clare.

"Why was that horse tied to a roll of fence wire?" was the first thing he asked.

"It had a saddle sore so they tied it back behind the barn because they couldn't let anybody ride it. Then when it heard the other horses going, it wanted to go along as it was used to doing," I told him.

"A lady down at the beach phoned the Manager to tell him the horse was there with the fence wire completely unrolled on the road," Fae rasped.

Her breathing was so labored and raspy, it could be heard in the next room. We felt we wanted to breathe for her. She couldn't change her position for the pain of that broken rib, the twisted cartilages, and the injured side. We went downstairs, sat on the chesterfield with our arms around each other and cried like a pair of babies.

Our Fae, so badly hurt! Would she recover completely? What would this do to her? We asked ourselves these questions and more! Since the pain did not subside, a week later she was taken to St. Mary's hospital for sun-ray lamp treatments. She remained there for a week, returned home and spent three more weeks in a hospital bed which I had rented from the Red Cross Society.

We didn't know we had so many friends until this accident happened. Telephone calls, cards, letters, and visitors overwhelmed us.

One of the first visitors who came to see us was Pat Bailey who cried fit to break her heart because she said, "It's all my fault. Fae didn't want to go riding and I pressed her to."

Aldean Reade of Elmira came to see Fae a few days after she arrived home and, as we stood on our front verandah for a few moments discussing what had happened, Aldean keeled over in a dead faint! Her brother arrived to take her home after a brief visit with Fae, a cup of hot tea and lunch.

It was through this accident that I became better acquainted with Helen Wesson, a neighbour who lived just around the corner at 12 Crescent Street, when her daughter June brought her in to see Fae. Our children had gone to Sheppard School together for several years. This has remained a pleasant and lasting friendship.

Fae finally improved enough to go back to her work at The Waterloo Trust and Savings Company office, but the broken rib continued to bother her. At the time, our family doctor did not approve of removing it, but preferred to let nature adjust it, although the surgeon said he could take it back part way and make her more comfortable.

If she dropped anything, she could not bend down to pick it up because the rib would flip off the breastbone, slap against her lung and take her breath away. She put up with this for almost two years when she decided that nature needed a little assistance, and the surgeon removed the offending rib.

During that two year period the strain of the accident and the extra work because of this handicap made us decide to secure a home on one floor and we moved to 70 Rosedale Avenue, shortly before the operation.

Chapter XIV

A Neighbourhood Romance

Several romances bloomed and faded for Fae previous to our move to 70 Rosedale Avenue. Then one day I noticed the young man who boarded next door squatting on his foot in our driveway talking to Clare. He had done this several times. Then one day it happened at a time when Fae was coming in from work. Clare introduced them and, before long, Jim and Fae were dating regularly. They were married August 19th, 1955, and Fae became Mrs. James A. Freure.

Our first granddaughter, Catherine Mary, was born on March 26th, 1957; the second one, Shannon Lynn, June 2nd, 1959. Catherine Mary was as pretty as a picture with her golden hair and brown eyes, and she showed her independence and versatility almost from the day she was born. A little mother from the time she was able to talk, she called herself "Mrs. Cooper" after she heard the name mentioned on a television commercial. Before she was four years old she had many of these commercials memorized and at five, she could harmonize to a melody.

This love of music has carried through the years until now at fourteen, she is considered a prodigy. All she has to do is to hear a piece of music on the radio or television and in a day or so she has mastered it all by ear!

"Mrs. Cooper" never liked toys but preferred her Mother's coffee pot or saucepans. Her curiosity led her to take everything apart to see what was inside. At fourteen, she is never happier than when she can help her father unplug a drain, carry bricks to rebuild the fire place, or run to the tool box for another wrench or screwdriver. When this work is done, she is equally as happy to help her Mother whip up a meal in those pots and pans that interested her right from her baby days.

Shannon Lynn was a cuddly little dumpling with big, dark eyes and black hair that stood up straight like a Cupie doll's, and the nurses in the hospital named her "the little Butterball."

She was always pleasant and easy to get along with and she likes to see other people happy. Her kind and thoughtful nature has gained her a host of friends. In fact, she bubbles over with the zest of life wherever she goes.

Like her sister Cathy, she loves music and sings like a nightingale.

In sports, her first love is water skiing.

While she preferred to play with toys rather than pots and pans at the age of twelve, her interest in cooking has become apparent, as she helps her mother peel potatoes, stir the gravy, or tastes a morsel of the roasted chicken when it comes from the oven!

Chapter XV

California Bound

It was in June of 1956 that we packed our new, two-tone Orchid color Dodge and wended our way toward California to spend our vacation. Our route was mapped out by the Oil Company, but we made no reservations ahead. We just took our chances for overnight accommodation. Our route took us by way of Detroit and after leaving the State of Michigan, we proceeded along Route 66 through Indiana into Illinois the first day, making stops every three hours to stretch our legs, eat, freshen up, and change drivers for the next lap of the journey. In the early evening, a Motel sign near the highway gave promise of "Food, fuel, and lodging, at reasonable rates," which was a welcome end to a five hundred mile drive.

Refreshed from a night's rest, we got an early start on the second lap of our journey down through Illinois, Missouri, and Oklahoma. Clare slept as I sped down the Oklahoma Freeway at eighty miles an hour with the face of the speedometer blazing "Red for danger," and the clock frowning five o'clock, "Time to put up for the night" if we wanted to be sure of a place to stay.

Clare woke up suddenly as I stopped the car to pay the toll before leaving the freeway. "Time to change drivers again," he said, as he slipped around the car to get into the driver's seat. I slid over and on we went to look for motel signs. It wasn't long before we saw one that claimed to have a high rating, but when we approached it we could see a "No vacancy" sign scribbled on a piece of cardboard which was stuck in the window.

"That's funny, their electric sign that shows from the highway says, Vacancy," I said.

"Oh, well, I guess it's easier for them to stick that sign in the window than it is to push a button on the electric sign! You come across a lot of that both in Canada and the United States," Clare answered.

As we left their premises to enter the traffic circle that would take us back onto the highway, there was a toll chute with its gaping jaws wide open to gobble up those nickels and dimes as fast as they were thrown into it. "Fifteen cents, please", the sign under the red light said. Fifteen cents we gave it in return for a green light and as we proceeded around the circle unable to find our proper outlet toward the south, we ended up face to face with that greedy monster the second time.

"Nothing to do but feed it again," said Clare, as he threw in another fifteen cents.

Around we went again and since there was no direction sign, we couldn't figure out which outlet went south, and once again we were face to face with "Old Ironsides" daring us to go through on a red light! Clare threw in the third fifteen cents as he swore he would take any highway that presented itself even if it pointed "north". It did! He went a few feet and slipped into the circle again and — you guessed it - the monster, the red light - another fifteen cents — green light!

"D'ya know something," he whined. "This could become a habit, if a fellow's not careful! Now if that highway went back toward the north, then the second outlet just has to go south, so I will take that one this time." At last we were out of the monster's clutches!

On we drove looking for motel accommodation and we soon found the ideal spot near an uncomplicated outlet from the highway near Clinton, Oklahoma. It was while staying at these motels that we had the best roast beef dinners we have ever tasted. The farther west we travelled, the nicer the beef became and we had many invitations to - "You all come back". It was in the west that the friendliness was contagious, and that the bigness was overwhelming. The quietness was eerie, and the sound of thunder had a hollowness that we had never heard before.

The third day as we entered the State of Texas I said, "I believe we just go through a corner of this state. We should soon hit New Mexico." We drove, drove, drove and drove morning, afternoon and evening until ten o'clock. We stopped for the night near Amarillo and the next day at the crack of dawn we started out again driving, driving, driving morning, afternoon and evening and we were still in the State of Texas.

"Gosh, Texas has awfully big corners," Clare said to the attendant where we stopped for gas. "My wife said we only had to cross one corner of Texas!"

"Texas has awfully big everything," a deep voice rumbled from beneath a cowboy hat that sat on top of this seven-foot Texan.

"Nearly dislocated my neck looking up at him," said six-foot Clare as we drove away with our car freshly serviced.

We stayed at a motel close-by that night and an early-morning start got us across the border into New Mexico by ten o'clock.

"I wonder when we go through the desert?" enquired Clare as I drove down the modern highway flanked by sand dunes, flowering cacti, and the odd picnic table and bench built of solid cement.

"We've been going through it for some time although with highways like this, you'd never know it. I wouldn't have guessed it but for those big things over there," I said, as I pointed to the Giant Saguaros, graceful Yucca (sometimes called Spanish Bayonet) and other desert wild flowers.

"What I'm wondering is when we will be going through the mountains? I've been watching them in the distance for some time, but we never seem to get any closer," I continued.

We barrelled along Route 66 that afternoon and evening stopping only for the usual meals and car service, and just before sundown the grey outline of the mountains suddenly burst into a myriad of colors. We gasped, we groaned, we revelled in the magnificence, the magnitude, the miracle of the spectacle that was before us! I felt diminished to the size of an ant as I tried to absorb the beauty and bigness of that panorama. It was the last thing we talked about as we retired that night, and the first thing we talked about in the morning!

"Fill 'er up," Clare told the attendant at the service station.

"Getting an early start this morning? Which way ya' headin', Mac?" (He didn't know his name was Clare!)

"We're on our way to Los Angeles," Clare answered.

"Ya' better put Ethyl in your car to go through them mountains. It's the altitude, ya' know. Lucky ya' have an eight cylinder car - lots of folks get stuck up there," the man continued.

"Should I have the carburetor adjusted?"

"Nope, just use Ethyl while you're in California, that's all ya' have to do. Have a good trip, folks," he said as he waved us on our way.

With Ethyl in our tank and my "Mac" re-christened husband at the wheel, we headed into the mountains to glory in miles and miles of breathtaking beauty in that gigantic patch-work quilt that seemed to cover the earth, broken here and there by the highway as it spiralled around the mountain like a silver ribbon and disappeared into one of the many tunnels along the route.

Along the way we saw some of the cars that didn't make it. Some with house trailers, too heavy for the overburdened car motors, stood abandoned on the shoulder of the highway. Blown out tires or remnants of them were strewn here and there giving evidence of the strain they had had speeding through the hundred and ten degree heat of the desert.

Tiny white crosses by the dozens planted all along the shoulder of the road told a story of others who didn't reach their destination. My niece, who had moved to California some years before, had told us the story of those white crosses. She told us that, as the engineers were excavating for the highway, they came across the graves of early settlers who died trying to get through the mountains with their covered wagons and that each one they disturbed was reburied at the side of the highway with a white cross to mark its position.

These crosses were only six to eight inches high, but they must have been revered by all motorists whether they understood their significance or not because we saw none of them damaged even though some of them were very close to the edge of the pavement.

We arrived at my niece's home late on the fifth day and stayed overnight with her and her family in Buena Park which is close to Los Angeles, and since her home is within walking distance of Knott's Berry Farm plans were made that evening for our first visit to that amusement centre.

Chapter XVI

Knott's Berry Farm and Ghost Town.

Walter Knott, Creator and owner of this eighty acre Berry Farm Museum and Ghost Town, started this enterprise on the farm he and his family pioneered.

It is set out in streets and trails just like a self-contained town, and no matter what you want to buy, you will find it in one of the thirty-three intriguing shops.

There is a Berry Market on the original little berry stand site where you can buy the products that made the farm famous. Their raspberry, strawberry, boysen-berry (a fruit obtained by crossing the raspberry, blackberry and loganberry) jams are all made without seeds or you could buy it with seeds if you wished.

The Rock & Book Shop showed books on the Old West, rare and out-of-print items, as well as beautiful specimen rocks and hand made jewelry.

The General Merchandise Store — what a store! We've never seen anything to compare with it. Every inch was crammed with old time merchandise. It even displayed old-fashioned penny candles.

The Antique Shop had jewelry, glass, Haviland, Victorian silver, and furniture, lovely remnants of the past that make perfect accents for our homes today.

Apparel for the ladies, little miss, and men, young and old, costume jewelry, and toys could be found in Marion & Toni's Sport Shop.

What a sparkling display there was in the Glass Blowers Store (1861) — fantasies in glass featured birds, animals, and figurines, designed for hobby or utility!

If you wished to try your skill on the target range with a gun or a bow and arrow, you could purchase your weapon at Harry's Gunshop.

For funny pictures, a supply of photo needs, or a camera rental, a visit to the "Pitchur Gallery" would solve your problem. A young couple sitting in a covered wagon drawn by two mules, with the words, "Ghost Town or Bust! !" written over their heads like a halo was one amusing pose that caught our attention.

The Candle Kitchen and Weaver's Parlour were in one building which was styled like an ordinary house with sun room and verandahs, and featured hand-dipped candles, prettied up with clusters of fruit or flowers, scented or plain, in the kitchen; and lovely hand-loomed bags, mats, and many styles of stoles and skirts, some woven of the popular metalic yarns, in the Parlour section.

In the Portrait Studio, skilled artists waited to make a pastel portrait of you with a few minutes sitting or from your favorite photograph.

The Knifemaker's Shop was busy making beautiful knives of every sort, from sportsmen's game and fish knives to utility types, all of the finest steel.

More than eighteen exotic lands provide the baskets sold in the Basket Shop. No end to the surprises in this one!

Red's Leather Works, a real leather shop, features name brands as well as hand-made articles and custom work. You can drop in and watch the craftsmen at work.

The Woodcraft Shop is stocked with woodcarvings from California and abroad, also Redwood, Myrtlewood, and unusual wood gifts and souvenirs.

The Train Supply House is one of the largest and most fabulous toy and train museums in the United States. There is also a complete line of toy trains, parts and service.

The shopper can watch beautiful pure wool socks being made on a very old British Rib Sock machine, in the Sock Makers Shop.

Three minutes is all they need in the Plastic Shack to seal any item from your wallet in plastic; your Social Security Card, Driver's License, favorite Photo or a Lock of Hair.

A glowing fairyland is portrayed in the Art Glow Studio and all the items are for sale at reasonable prices. This is one of the most unique of the Farm shops.

Even the coin and stamp collector is not forgotten at Knott's Berry Farm. The advertisement at the Miner's Bank reads, "Coin and Stamp Collections, bought, sold, or exchanged."

Aside from a treasure trove of gift items, there's an unlimited selection of costume jewelry, perfumes, and greeting cards in the Virginia Gift Shop.

Go up the trail to Ghost Town and you could see the gold mine where you can pan your own gold! An old-timer shows you how, and it's real gold too. You'll enjoy this authentic old gold mine.

Historic cable cars from San Francisco carry you through the grounds, with all the clang and clatter of yesteryears, to the seal pool, the observatory, and Old MacDonald's barn yard, where a continuous show of animal acts is in progress. When we went by this barn yard, a Billy goat was balancing himself precariously near the edge of the roof as he tossed a tin can into the air and caught it again. Also in the barn yard, you can have a ride on a hundred year old mule-powered merry-go-round.

Take the stage road to the Calico Saloon and you will see the jazz-gartered leg of a naughty lady hanging out of the upstair window! Over to the left we stopped to examine the one-room jail, popular in the west a century ago, with its lanky prisoner in effigy.

A loud voice said, "Where did you get that bald headed old goat lady? Hey, Baldy, did you have to rob the cradle?" We couldn't see any evidence, but we figured the actors were planted up in the Calico Saloon and had a microphone in the head of the make-believe prisoner.

Nearby, waiting to thrill you, is the Haunted Shack with its "truly incredible, amazing, amusing confusing, but not frightening atmosphere, where even scientists are puzzled. Men, women and childen enjoy this 'ghostliest' place in Ghost Town." Or walk across School Road to the old school, with a real school teacher standing in the doorway, dressed in the clothes of her time! In front of it is the Bird Cage Theatre "where a well-known cast of players will delight you with hilarious performances of old-time melerdramers, and where you can cheer the hero, or hiss the villain!"

"The Pride of Ghost Town" is a mile long railway that takes you around the mountain, over the trestle that spans Gold Gulch, and back to the depot.

You can walk the trails or ride the cable cars to see the old church, the chapel, the Indian Village, the lake with hand-hewn canoe, and petland.

On the corner of Indian Village Trail and Gold Mine Road there is a Covered Wagon Camp where the covered wagons which belonged to the folks "that made it through the mountains" are preserved for posterity One fleeting moment of reverence captured us as we remembered the little white crosses that we had seen along the mountain highway a few days before.

Children were delighted with the burro rides. The animals were gentle, the rides long, and careful attendants made this one of the happiest features for youngsters.

Grown-ups enjoyed the stage coach rides where they captured the thrill of horse and buggy days "in a real old, old stage coach or covered wagon, drawn by beautiful horses at a lively clip."

On the verandah of one of the buildings, a little old lady, who claimed to be over a hundred years old (and you could believe it), played one of only two harmoniums purported to be left in the world.

Restaurants, Grill, rest rooms, parking lots, first aid, Steak House, Bakery, Garden Room, Chicken Dining Room, Juice Stand, Nursery. You name it — Knott's Berry Farm has it in its eighty-acre wonderland!*

* Much of this material can be found in the brochure of Knott's Berry Farm.

Chapter XVII

The Grand Canyon.

Grand Canyon National Park is part of that priceless heritage of the United States preserved "for the benefit and enjoyment of the people" in the National Park System. "The canyon is a titanic gorge, 4 to 18 miles wide, 217 miles long, cut by the mighty Colorado River as it rushes to the sea. Rising from its depths are rims and mountains, reaching a mile toward the sky. Over the rock temples and into the depths of the chasm spreads a veil of ever-changing colors."

Watching from the South Rim in the morning, when the light slants lengthwise from the Painted Desert, one sees the great capes of the opposite rim suddenly outlined in golden light against which their shapes loom in hazy blues. Down in the gorge, here and there, stretches of the Colorado River reflect in the sunlight.

An hour later all is changed. The dark capes are brilliant-hued and well-defined. Scores of new temples have emerged from the purple gloom.

At midday the opposite walls have flattened and the capes and temples have lost their definite shadows. But as the afternoon wears on the spectacles of the morning creep back, now reversed and strangely altered in outline.

At sunset, the reds deepen to dim purples and the grays and yellows and greens change to magical blues.

Then night falls, and in the dark the Canyon suggests unimaginable mysteries. But should there be a moon, the outlines of the great abyss revive in silver light, a thousand spectral forms projected from inscrutable gloom."

Since the length of our vacation did not permit it, and since riding a donkey three thousand feet down into the bowels of the earth was not one of our secret ambitions, we did not take the two-day trip into the Canyon, but had to be content with what we could learn about it from people who had just returned or by reading pamphlets available on the subject.

"Exploring the Grand Canyon by descending the trails to its innermost vastness is a memorable experience. The trip is usually made by muleback in parties led by experienced guides."

"Hikers should make inquiry at the park office before attempting the canyon trips. The trip to the Colorado River and return is very strenuous and one's ability should not be over-estimated. Food and water should be carried."

"There are two splendid trails from the South Rim to the Colorado River, and in the bottom of the canyon another trail along the river connects the two trails. The Bright Angel Trail trip is the one most frequently taken . Every turn in this famous, well-built trail opens up new vistas, each seemingly more spectacular than the one before. About half-way down a stop is made at Indian Gardens, after which the trail stretches out upon the Tonto Plateau and presently heads downward through the Granite Gorge to the rocky banks of the turbulant Colorado. After a stop for luncheon, the return journey is made and the arrival at the rim is in late afternoon."

After we left the Grand Canyon, on Highway 15, we had not gone far when we noticed a helicopter which had landed near the highway and several airmen and police officers were looking around the area. One of them waved at us to stop!

"Must be an accident or something," Clare said, as we both got out of the car.

Did you people see two planes collide in the air?" enquired the officer.

"No," we replied in unison!

"We were informed that two planes collided, and one witness said they landed in the Grand Canyon. Wondered if you had seen them," he said as he thanked us, instructed us to go ahead, and proceeded to wave down a car that approached behind us.

A few days later radio reports told us the grim story of the discovery of the wrecked passenger planes in the canyon, with no survivors.

A short time later we heard another report which told of the finding of a young couple on a ledge in the Grand Canyon. The man was dead, but the girl was still alive but badly injured. They had gone over the edge of the Canyon in their car nine days before. When we compared dates, we figured that they were down there the day we visited the Canyon.

We continued on highway 15 towards Las Vegas where we stayed overnight, had a hcance to view the spectacle of a city that never sleeps, and where the brilliance from millions of lights turns night into sunny day as business buzzes around the clock with slot machines, roulette wheels, bingo ball shakers, fancy ladies in off-the-shoulder dresses, and gentlemen flicking the ashes off expensive cigars!

We had breakfast in the restaurant of the Golden Nugget Gambling Hall, but we didn't have the thrill of trying a bit of gambling, since the Canadian Government, at that time, did not allow us to take enough money out of the country to play a game of "Penny Ante".

ONT

Chapter XVIII

The Short Cut!

A visit to California and the Grand Canyon over, our thoughts and our car pointed homeward — two thousand miles to go.

With luck, no car trouble, and my husband and me alternating the driving, we will make it in five days.

A cross-road bears upon us, a welcome service station on the far right side with gasoline pumps to quench the thirst of our car's gas tank. "Yes, sir. Fill 'er up, please!"

As the nostril-stinging liquid poured from the automatic pump into the gluttonous gas tank, the attendant checked the oil, the battery, cleaned the windshield, and chattered away. "Where ya' head'n' today, folks?"

"We're heading for Salt Lake City," Clare told him.

"There's really not much up there to see. Why don't you go that way?" he said, pointing his finger to the road on the right.

"You will see much more that way — the Indian Reserve — much more interesting that way; goes right through to Green River — will save you two hundred and fifty miles."

The car check-up completed, its gas tank replenished, we headed east toward the Indian Reserve and Green River. The highway was like any other highway for about twenty-five miles and then things changed. It narrowed into a one-lane, silt-covered path, bounded on the left by heaven-high mountains of ghastly grey rock; on the other, by a depth of nothingness.

At the bottom of this chasm, the Colorado River seemed just a silver thread. One false move and the car would be swallowed in its gaping jaws. A piece of rock fell in front of our car — it looked flat — the car passed over it. It wasn't flat enough and the noise of rock against metal resounded in our ears.

A one-lane path winding through the mountains of rock — no room to meet another car — a sharp curve — the sound of an engine louder than our own — the clatter of steel against stones — two big eyes glaring at us. We were face to face with a road-grader.

The operator motioned to us to stay where we were. There was a cave behind his machine. He twisted the steering wheel this way and that, and backed the grader into the cave so that we could get by. We continued our hazardous journey.

Up, up, miles upgrade; down, down, miles downgrade; curves to the left, curves to the right, then into clearing. Are we on the moon? On television the moon looks like that grey rock — acres of awesome grey rock. The road had died a few miles back; nothing but the faint evidence of car tracks.

How much farther must we go until we reach Green River? Will our gasoline hold out? Perhaps we should turn back. Will the gas hold out if we do? No road signs, no road — speed limit dictated by the curves, the narrowness of the ledge, the depth of the precipice on the right. The walls of rock disappear — the tracks of two cars show up — one on the left, the other veering to the right. Two rough boards form a cross protruding from the rocks. "Uranium Mines" and "Green River" were pencilled across it with directional arrows. Saved by the arrow! We obeyed it!

The clearing ended and we re-entered those towering walls of rock. The sky darkened — thunder rolled — rain fell — another treacherous curve — a man and a small boy rested in a parked car watching the flash-flood of water tearing down over the only access to civilization.

"Don't try to go through it", the man warned — "We have lost several cars that way — you'd never be found. We've slept in the car all night waiting for the water to subside."

My husband examined the situation — it didn't look that bad to him — so we proceeded along our way, sliding, slithering on the greasy silt, yanking and twisting the car wheel to keep on the narrow ledge of the mountain. Our minds more at ease, we hoped to be out of the mountains before dark. The road widened — we met a car with two men in it. The driver slowed down.

"How is it up at the wash?" he yelled.

Informed that we had just come through it — they went on their way; we, on ours.

An old frame house came into view on the left side of the road. It had a tiny garden formed in the hollow of the rock. Surely we must be getting close to Green River. Down, down hill — the road widening still more into a two-lane highway. The lifeless remains of a rattlesnake lay six feet long on the roadway. A few miles farther on, we found a general store — Indians lazing on chairs outside. We drove close to the window and could see women busy inside, children playing on the floor, groceries piled on the shelves, and a pot-bellied stove in the middle of the room.

Along the foot of the mountains were flimsy shacks — the homes of the Indians. We met several of them riding horses — men, women and children. There were a few riderless ponies with them, each with its front feet tied together with rope so that it would not stray from the others. The plight of those "three-legged" ponies was pitiful to us. They took two steps with the hind legs and then hopped forward with the manacled forelegs. Before we were far up the road, we saw them turn into one of the small farms.

This was the Indian Reserve our friend at the gas station had mentioned. Miles of shacks -- unfit for human habitation. Iron kettles hung from tressles over the ashes of still smouldering fires. A small plot of corn was growing in the field — their leaves waving us on toward our goal — Green River.

Upgrade for ten miles — downgrade for six miles — through mountainous rock — out into another clearing — another flash-flood — the valley, a small lake — the highway covered with water. We ploughed through and soon another general store and service station appears. Our gas did hold out! We had the damaged pan examined by the mechanic.

"You're pretty lucky, sir — one inch to the right and you would have broken the steering rod!"

"One mile to Green River", answered the attendant to our query. That mile was a long mile — the whole trip that day was just one hundred and fifty miles but it took a five-hour-eternity. A motel on the main highway just south of Green River gave us shelter for the night. We wondered, as we rested, how many people our friend back at the crossroads had sent through this "interesting" death trap. We saved two hundred and fifty miles straight ahead, but we went three hundred up and down.

ONIONS

Chapter XIX

The Last Lap.

As we followed Highway 70 on the way to Denver, Colorado, where the mountains changed from their depressing grey rocks to restful green trees and shrubs, we decided to further conserve our depleting funds by picnicking along the way. This is where I almost came to grief when we walked into a shack that protruded from a hole in the side of the mountain, which the owner dared to call a "store", and asked a t-a-a-ll man with a Texas accent "if he had any SPANISH onions".

"Nope, lady, them's not Spanish onions, them there's TEXAS onions," he beamed, as he gave his sleeping partner a kick on the shins to let him know they had a customer!

The other fellow limped from his chair, half-dazed, and stood beside us and the basket of onions.

"Pick yourselves a pur-r-ty one," he whined as he rubbed his leg and looked daggers at his wakener.

With our "pur-r-ty onion", that Clare picked, a cucumber, some tomatoes, and a couple of thick slices of meat (cut by a Texan, remember) we left the store to have our picnic.

We carried bread, butter, soda biscuits, cookies and water in the car for emergencies, so we then had the makings of a healthy "Dagwood sandwich".

We found a picnic area a short distance away where we stopped to eat. Since we had been sitting so much in the car, we strolled around the table and trees munching our sandwiches as the juices they emitted ran down our forearms and dripped from our elbows.

"Boy, that was some ride through the Indian Reserve to Green River! I was scared to death! Were you?"

"I sure was, but I didn't want you to see it!" Clare answered. "The thing I feared most was that we might run out of gas, and I hadn't the slightest idea how far we were from a gas station! I'd never go through there again! Always better to stick to the bigger highways," he continued.

"When those mountains are wet, it's like driving on lard! Far worse than driving on ice at home. At least you can get some traction with your snow tires, but when that silt is wet on the mountains, you have no control whatsoever."

A spring water pump at the picnic area provided not only a refreshing drink, but also a cooling slush for our face and arms before we continued our journey homeward.

The only other point-of-interest we visited was Yellowstone National Park, where we gazed in awe at the geysers, sneaked slowly past an extinct volcano, lest the vibration of our car might make it come alive and erupt over us and the panoramic beauty of the district, and where we viewed beautiful Yellowstone Lake and the wild bird and animal refuge.

As we headed through Wyoming, Nebraska, Iowa, and on to the Canadian Border in our two-tone Orchid Dodge, stopping only for night lodging, meals, re-fueling the car, we came to the conclusion that one can get very tired of travelling through mountains; that the American people are friendly and hospitable; that the roast beef gets better the farther west you go; that Texas is as big as they say it is; that you just don't ask a Texan if he is selling SPANISH onions; that we enjoyed our holiday very much, and that, if we accepted all the invitations we received from the restaurant owners that "Y'all come back", we would certainly have to take up permanent residence in the United States!

Chapter XX

Rest-Eze.

Since we had seen every State in the Union, except four, and since our daughter Fae worried about us when we were on the highways, we decided to buy a cottage at Wasaga Beach and furnish it with a couple of ROCKING CHAIRS!

On May 31st, 1958, our deal was closed and we were the proud owners of Rest-Eze cottage on Pine Drive, Wasaga Beach, Ontario. The cost was twenty-three hundred dollars. It was built into a hill. The front half sat on solid ground and the back end was supported by several seven-foot stilts, a couple of which leaned at a Tower of Pisa angle.

The cottage consisted of a living-room-kitchen combination, two small bedrooms and a one-piece bathroom which appeared to have baen added as an afterthought since it was built over the back verandah and door, which left only the front door of the cottage for ingress or egress.

The living-room-kitchen was furnished with a day-bed, two wicker chairs, a wood stove with a pipe that went straight up through the peak of the roof, a two-burner electric stove, the kind where you use half of this burner and half of that burner, and if you use either one, you can't use the oven, a Norge refrigerator which, judging by the noise it made, must have been the first one off the asembly line when refrigerators were invented. (We named it "Vesuvius" because it was always erupting). There was also a maple table with two benches and a cabinet to match. The first five articles had seen better days, but the maple outfit had been hand-made by the man who built the cottage and seemed to be the eye-catcher to a prospective buyer. (It threw me!) Each bedroom had a brown tubular iron bed, a dresser, and a chair. The floors throughout were covered with patterns of linoleum that looked like the vintage of three different eras.

The first evening we spent in the place was a rainy one, and as we sat in the living-room looking the situation over, the rain poured down the stove pipe into the stove, and near the front door another stream pelted down into a dishpan which I had found among the TREASURES in the kitchen cupboard. As the rain diminished, the whish-sh of the water dropping into the woodfire, the intermittent kaplink of the raindrops hitting the dishpan, combined with the clang of a tree limb which the wind lashed against the eavestrough and the ungodly squeals from the refrigerator as its motor started, we had a four-piece orchestra lending assistance to the faint strains of The Blue Danube on the radio!

As my eyes wandered from the dripping stove pipe — to the dishpan half-full of water in the front doorway — to the old wood-stove — the creaky, wicker rocking chair Clare was sitting in — and wondered what we had got into now, our eyes met in a questioning glance that seemed to betray our thoughts to one another.

"What the devil have we got into now?" Clare said.

"I dunno, guess we should have looked at it on a rainy day," I chuckled.

"We might as well go to bed, nothing we can do tonight anyway. I'll look at the roof in the morning to see what can be done," Clare lamented.

I was the first in bed and, as Clare walked across the kitchen to turn out the lights and returned to the back bedroom, the cottage shimmied on its posts. "Better step lightly, boy, or this thing will slide down the bank," I yelled.

"Lots of work to do around here. It will take time, but it's a start, and we'll make a nice place out of it", were the words that echoed from the next room.

Make a nice place of it, we did, and it took plenty of time and money. We sold the contents of the living-room-kitchen except that maple dinette suite that had snared me to the Community Auction Centre for four dollars and fifty cents. With the pot-bellied stove and its wandering pipes, the electric stove with its broken burners, 'Vesuvius', the refrigerator, the daybed and woodbox out of the way, the contractor had access to repair the leaking roof, line the cottage, install ceilings throughout, and build cupboards across the back-end of the kitchen complete with a stainless steel sink.

Then we purchased a new studio couch, an automatic electric stove, a Frigidaire with a freezer, a portable television, a chair or two, and I hung a few pictures which I had saved from the weekly newspaper over a period of years, in hopes that some day we might own a cottage. Then the plumber installed a wash basin in the bathroom.

All these improvements made quite a transformation, but we had retained the bedroom furniture and those high-backed tubular beds bugged me. I thought about them all week at home and decided that I would improve that eyesore when we went up to the cottage the next weekend! We spruced up the dressers and chairs with a coat of paint to match the beds and while Clare was up on the roof removing the moss that had accumulated over the years I decided to carry out my brain-wave to improve those beds. I thought to myself — I'll turn the bottom end to the top and cut off the higher end to form a Hollywood bed!

Butterflies fluttered in my stomach as I rushed to the tool box for the metal saw. Gotta get this done while Clare's up on the roof, I thought, or he might object. I sawed away at the one side and after what seemed like an eternity, the metal saw lopped it off.

Then I proceeded to saw the other side, but when I got half way through the tube, the bed, box spring and mattress collapsed pinning me against the wall! I had sawed below the supporting rod instead of above it, and the legs buckled knock-kneed style! Just couldn't let Clare see me in this position! I'd never live it down! I reached for a dresser drawer as my knees held the bed from dropping all the way down, yanked it out, turned it on its side for extra height, placed it under the bed and wiggled myself out of my precarious position.

Just as I extricated myself, the front door opened and there stood Clare gazing at the Hollywood bed that didn't quite make it! "Guess I made a boo-boo," I said guiltily.

"You sure did," he quipped, as he examined the situation. "But, never mind, we'll take the end of the bed back to Kitchener to have it welded."

I ended up with my modernized bed in the one room, but the other one was left in its original state!

When all the inside work was completed, we painted the outside of the cottage white, with shutters and steps in Terracotta red, a rich, deep red — not that bright red you see on barns. Then we hung our new name plate at the left corner, extending it past the end of the cottage to make it more readable from the street. This name plate was a wrought iron one that I had made from one side of the frame of a Raymond sewing machine which I had picked up along the highway one Sunday as we drove home to Kitchener.

We were clipping it off at quite a speed that day, but as we passed a spot where the Highway Department had bulldozed a hill back to widen the road, I noticed this iron thing with a name on it and I exclaimed to Clare, "Stop a minute, there's something over there with our name on it!" I hurried over and, as I got closer to it, I could see the name was "Raymond" — not "Hammond". I took it back to the car and as we continued our journey homeward, my brain immediately set to work figuring how to make a name-plate for the cottage out of it.

The following week I cut away at it with the metal saw, removing the superfluous legs, casters and curlicues, and ended up with a crest-shaped doo-dad that I knew just had to be the envy of all the cottage owners on Pine Drive, provided I could change that name to "Hammond". There were only two letters between me and success, the R and the Y, so I cut the rounded top out of the

R and the bottom part off the Y and formed them into an H and an M with plastic wood, and then I painted the whole thing over with black paint for contrast against the white cottage.

People eyed the place! Such remarks as, "The Doll's House", "Now all you need to do is to change that Rest-Eze to Never Finished", were some of the remarks the neighbours made as they strolled by. No truer words were ever spoken than "never finished", for after having weekend guests a few times, we decided to add an addition to the cottage to make extra sleeping space.

The addition contained a ten by twelve-foot bedroom, an L-shaped hall, and a back door which opened onto a verandah. We covered the floors with new inlaid linoleum. We furnished the bedroom with a second-hand dresser, a chair and twin beds, which we made from a couple of doors that Clare's brother removed from the farmhouse when they made an archway between their living-room and dining-room.

The doors were made of Georgia Pine. Since they were seven feet, six inches long we had to shorten them by one foot, and since each bed was to have six legs, we measured and marked twenty-four spots on each bed where the screws were to go to attach the fixtures that held the legs in place. As Clare drilled the holes for the first bed, I attached the metal pieces and screwed the legs in place. Then as we turned it over to make room to work on the second one, I noticed the new linoleum was full of perforations! The drill not only went through the door, but also went through our new linoleum! We placed the second door on blocks for the drilling operation and with the addition of a couple of head boards, a couple of coats of paint, and two of the best mattresses made by the Waterloo Bedding Company, we had a pair of twin beds second to none.

With the inside of the cottage finished at last, our thoughts turned to improving the grounds around it. We put steps in the bank to go up to the front door, steps in the back bank to go down to the basement room and the garden, planted one hundred evergreen trees we scrounged from along the highways where the roads were being widened and the bulldozers were grinding them into the earth. Mingled with our full-grown oaks, pines and basswoods, the setting gave relaxation not only to us and our guests, but also delighted the many families of squirrels, chipmunks, and birds that hovered around.

We loved to accommodate those little friends in our trees and crannies outside the cottage, but we did resent it when we went up to the cottage one weekend and found that the saucy little rascal of a squirrel had chewed the label and part of the back out of Clare's nineteen dollar sweater coat that Fae and Jim had given him for Christmas. How the squirrel got to it, we'll never know, since the rod on which it hung was attached to the cement wall at each end and was stretched across the corner of the room. Clare suggested it might have carried a parachute to drop down from the ceiling! We know it was a squirrel that perpetrated the crime because we saw his droppings on the rod. We never knew which one did it, but we were sure it couldn't have been "Greedy Gut", because he was always so full of peanuts the Bidgood children fed him to want to eat the label off a sweater. The children named him "Greedy Gut" because he would eat peanuts out of their hands until he swelled up like a balloon and could hardly wobble back to his hole in the oak tree.

That oak and the three pines at the front of the cottage shimmered like shot-silk on a moonlight night or when the front light was turned on, and often their acorns and cones would pelt the roof on a windy night. That is why we couldn't bring ourselves to cut the oak down when we enlarged the cottage even though it meant cutting the size of the new bedroom down.

In the spring of the year, when we opened the cottage, the ground would be two inches thick with pine needles and as we raked them up in the brisk air of late March our nostrils and lungs tingled with the refreshing, pine-scented air.

One day Clare came home with the news that changes were to be made in the district. The plan our neighbour had shown him had the street near our cottage marked as a new entrance to the beach and the large property across the street was to be a parking lot. All our dreams of a quiet weekend retreat came crashing down around us. Seven years of work, building, rebuilding, improvising and repairing, crushed by the giant-foot of progress like an ant hill under the foot of a picnicker!

On May twenty-eighth, 1965, our cottage was sold fully furnished, including the two ROCKING CHAIRS, and once again we were "Knights of the Road", our daughter's fears for our safety notwithstanding.

Chapter XXI

White Serpents flew by our Window.

The adjustment wasn't easy for we missed those weekend trips to the "Doll's House". But there were certain compensations especially from a financial standpoint. Keeping up two homes for two people was a costly business, to say nothing of the seven-day work week we put in to care for both places. In that respect, the cottage always seemed to have a slight edge on the home in Kitchener, and so when we got rid of it we turned our full attention to making some improvements at home.

The house had been built of cement block, covered with stucco facing, which defied even the most ingenious paint manufacturer to invent a product that would stay on more than one season. Sick to death of looking at our polka-dot house, and sheets of paint the size of saucers lying on the lawn, we decided to have the house covered with aluminum siding. We called two companies for estimates and the one we chose claimed to be giving a special discount for the month of March to round up business to prevent laying off their men during the slack season.

First thing in the morning, on March 16th, the men arrived with a truck load of siding and piled it on the front lawn. These siding strips were twelve feet long, about eight inches wide and were packed four to a box with white papers between the strips to prevent them scratching one another in transit. Then, after they prepared the house on the driveway side with a network of narrow slats, they inserted a Donnaconna board into each aluminum strip before they attached it to the house. By five o'clock that afternoon, they had that side finished and as they prepared to leave for home the boss said they would not be back the next day but would return the day after that to continue the work. "But when we signed the contract, Mr. Abelson said you would not leave the job once it was started. I purposely brought that stipulation up because we had an experience with a plumber a few years before when they started to put in our softener, and then left us for three weeks without any hot water to go on another job," I told him.

"Well, we have to do a job in Toronto, or we'll lose the contract," he said.

I rushed into the house to look up our contract and found that there was nothing in it to stop them leaving if they wished. I had to give in, but they promised again that they would not skip more than one day.

Soon after they had left, I saw Clare coming in the driveway and, as he stood there looking at the completed side of the house, I noticed that his face was drawn and that he looked exceptionally tired. We had our supper and since Grace Sisson, my neighbour was having our Church Group in for their March meeting, I went over at eight o'clock, leaving Clare resting from his trying day at the office. When I returned from the meeting about ten forty-five, he was pacing the floor complaining of a pain in his chest.

I went to the phone to call Dr. Watson, got no answer, and as I was trying again and again to get him, Clare went to the kitchen and took a dose of baking soda. I knew that Dr. Watson had been in Florida, but on my third try he answered the phone. When I told him how Clare had been acting and that, at the moment, he was spinning around in bed like a top, he said, "Give him an enema to take the gas down and I'll be right out!" I said, "I did give him one." "Give him another then," he said as he hung up the receiver.

I called Grace Sisson, who is a registered nurse, and since she was cleaning up the dishes from our meeting, she was still dressed and soon leaped over the hedge and into our house. She took over and gave Clare the second enema, while Dr. Watson was rushing from Waterloo to our place in the east end of Kitchener. He arrived in less than twenty minutes. (He came so fast, he forgot his dentures!)

When he saw Clare, he gave him a hypodermic and some diluted liquor. Then he walked out to the kitchen. As he did so Grace slipped out of the bedroom and said, "He wants some baking soda."

The doctor said, quietly, "Oh, no, that would kill him." Then he saw the baking soda on the counter! "He didn't take any of that, did he?"

I told him he had, while I was trying to get him on the phone, and he said, "Never give baking soda, it makes the gas backfire on the heart and kills more people than enough. Invariably, when we get a call and it's a heart attack, we find the baking soda on the table, and the person dead."

Clare's head, shoulders, arms and legs to the knees were like blocks of ice, and the Doctor and Grace Sisson stayed with him until three the next morning when he started to revive enough to be moved to the hospital. He was placed in the Intensive Care Unit at St. Mary's Hospital and after I had answered the questions at the desk the attendant took Clare's bag from me and led the way to the elevator to show me where he was. "Don't let the Intensive Care Unit bother you, they always put them in there as a precaution. Doesn't mean a thing," he said.

That was awfully nice of him, but he didn't fool me for one minute! I knew how bad Clare was! Five days later, as Fae and I came down the elevator with several nurses and other visitors, one nurse whispered to the other, "My coronary patient is just out of the woods, probably will go out of I.C. tomorrow."

Fae said later, "Did you hear what she said? That was Dad she was talking about."

Next day, he was changed to a semi-private room.

On the home front, the men did not return when they said they would. In between my morning and evening visits to the hospital, I telephoned the manager to see when they were coming. I reminded him that he had promised, before we signed the contract, that once the job was started it would not be left until it was finished.

Apparently they must have told other people the same thing for they didn't turn up at our place until the end of the week, and then only after some pretty hot conversations on the telephone, my end of which would not be considered ladylike in the best circles.

I watched them as they got busy once again placing the insulation boards into the aluminum, throwing the twelve foot strips of paper into a pile, fastening the strips to the side of the house, and then prepared to make my morning visit to the hospital, when suddenly the sky clouded over, a high wind roared, and all I could see were long, white serpents flying past the windows, the three men running here and there, grabbing at them and stuffing them under a box! I knocked three times on my forehead to make sure I was awake, and then, realizing that I had been a staunch teetotaler all my life, I sniffed at my teacup to make sure it had not been spiked by a gremlin fresh from old Ireland — and I realized that the pile of streamers from the aluminum sections had taken off for parts unknown!

I raced outside and the whole section looked as if it had been decorated for an outdoor wedding big enough to outdo any garden party ever held at Buckingham Palace! There were streamers in the trees, on the shrubs, wrapped around telephone and hydro poles, hanging from the eavestrough, skittering down Rosedale Avenue, twisting around the corner of Sheldon Avenue, and the neighbour's beagle hound, Chummy, who peered sadder-looking than usual, from under the one that was draped around her neck.

It was a strange March day, for the wind lasted an hour or so and then went down as suddenly as it had come up.

When the men saw that I was picking up papers, they stopped helping with them and went back to their jobs of house-covering. I put two large cartons out for them to put the rest of the streamers in, anchored them with heavy stones and placed them in a handy spot . Then I rushed up to the hospital to see Clare, but I didn't say a thing to him about what had happened.

The next day the men returned to work on the last side of the house. The boxes were filled to overflowing with streamers but, instead of packing them down so that the boxes could be closed, they kept throwing them on top or on the ground around them, and the same thing happened as the day before.

The trees leaned over with the sudden force of the wind, the men tugged at their jackets for all they were worth, and the streamers took off for the second time! Since the men were anxious to get the house finished by the weekend, they didn't bother picking them up.

They left it all for me.

I climbed over the fence into Mr. Foell's garden, through ankle-deep mud, up his peach tree, grabbed some streamers, back over the fence; vaulted the four-foot hedge into Sisson's garden, gathered them up from there; chased a couple racing neck and neck down Rosedale Avenue; met a car half-way down the block sucking one against its grill, narrowly missing a head-on collision with the same car! Almost gave the postman a hernia as he jumped out of my way and over-balanced with his heavy load of mail! I struggled back into a head-wind to put each armful into the boxes and jumped on them so that the tops would close and tied them with ropes. I gave the men a garbage can for the last few streamers, and I instructed them to pack them down and put the lid on OR ELSE! By the time I got up to the hospital that day, I was a candidate for the Intensive Care Unit myself!

Clare spent four-and-a-half weeks in the hospital and by the time he came home, we had a spanking white house, with green awnings, and trim, where he could relax his mind and body until he was able to return to his position at the City Hall. It wasn't until he was well on the way to recovery that I told him about the times the white serpents flew by our window!

Chapter XXII

The Plague of Repairmen.

From the time we started to gussy up our Kitchener home, we were plagued with breakages and repairs so that it seemed as if we were going two steps forward and three back. First of all I broke my partial plate; then I closed my hand in the car door and broke a claw off my diamond ring. For two years our eight hundred dollar, self-defrosting, refrigerator-freezer would not defrost in the freezer section. Several phone calls to the store where we purchased it brought the retort that "It isn't supposed to be self-defrosting." The pamphlets that came with it said it was self-defrosting, and several service calls proved that their service man didn't know how to repair it, but he said he would have the head maintenance man from the factory in London come up to look at it.

"You can't fool him on these things. He has been with the company since the first refriges were made and he knows every phase of the business," he assured me.

Several weeks later, Mr. "Lifelong Experience" arrived along with the service man and, after he removed the pile-up of ice that had formed on the bottom shelf, he took the food out, placed it in the kitchen sink, removed the wall-sections of the freezer to expose the wiring and there he had it!

"You see those two wires?" he said to the service man, as he pointed his finger deep into the works. "Those two wires are touching one another and when the defrosting operation starts the hot wire causes it to cut off too soon and the machine starts to refreeze before the ice is all off. They must have tipped the refrig. over too far when they carried it in from the store."

Then, with a complacent look on his face, he proceeded to re-assemble our freezer's innards. With an assuring shake of my hand and a face full of smiles, he and the service man left.

About thirty days later when I opened the freezer to get something off the bottom shelf, I noticed the ice had piled up again! I phoned the local service-man to tell him that they hadn't found the trouble after all. He informed me that the head office had been moved to Galt and that Mr. Fixit had been made manager of the new Company.

The next day I decided to see if Mr. Williams, the Waterloo service man for the same company, would look the situation over. When he came that day, he wasn't in the kitchen more than two minutes when he found the source of the trouble. He put his finger down into the small drain pipe where the water was supposed to escape into the evaporator pan and pulled out the plastic pipe that had turned up its ends to such a degree that it was causing the water to dam up, flow back into the freezer and there re-freeze.

"Nothing but the inferior material they are using today," he said, as he crumbled the pipe in his hands like a piece of bread and handed it to me to examine it. Then he pulled out the rest of the pipe and installed a new one, and our refrigerator has worked perfectly ever since.

Then one day we had to have the plumber to unblock the toilet. He emptied the water out of it, removed it from its moorings, took it out on the back lawn and cleaned out the sediment that had formed from the hard water. When he was replacing it, I saw him look at his watch, and soon he made a bee-line for the back door. I went into the bathroom to clean up the mess and found the toilet had not been cemented down as when he found it. I called his office and told them and they sent him back to finish the job. Fae had been home on her early lunch hour when he started to work on it in the first place and she whispered to me, "Throw that glass away in the bathroom; the plumber used it to empty the water out of the toilet!"

The following week the bill arrived! We were charged for a service call in the morning and another one in the afternoon, both portal to portal, when it would have taken only two minutes to have slapped some fresh goo on it to finish the job in the morning. We paid the bill and changed our plumber!

Later on our stationary tubs sprang a leak, and we had to have new ones installed. The new firm sent an elderly gentleman to do the work. Since the old tubs were cement it took a whole day to chop them out in pieces. After the new ones were in and the plumber had left, I decided to do some washing and found that his new stationary tubs leaked like a sieve around the plug hole. I called the office and they sent him back again. He adjusted it and it worked fine, but when I got the bill there was a charge of eight dollars and fifty cents for coming back to make their own new stationary tubs stop leaking. I went to their office immediately to pay the bill and when I showed it to the manager, he said, "He can't do that," and he struck it off to adjust the bill.

Next thing I knew my dryer wouldn't work. I called for a service man. They sent a tall, dark and handsome young fellow. Immediately he said, "Needs a new switch." He pulled off the vent pipe, yanked the dryer out from the wall, put in the new switch, jumped it back to the wall as if it was worth ten cents, grabbed the vent pipe, swung it around, smashed the light bulb above his head, didn't even say he was sorry, rammed the pipe back where it belonged and away he went. Two days later, I received the bill:

> "Checked dryer & found door switch defective. Replaced door switch & checked — all o.k. 61-0261 - Door Switch - $2.25, Tax .11. Service call $7.50. Labor $5.00. Pay this amount - $14.86."

That same day I went over to pay it and as I did so I asked the Manager what the five dollar labor charge was for when they made a service call charge of $7.50 and he informed me that the service call covers only the first fifteen minutes which they count from the time they leave their office and that time would be practically used up by the time they reached my door!

The following Monday when I tried to dry my washing, the machine wouldn't make a peep. When I called them back I instructed them to send a service man who knew something and not that ruffian who came the first time. That afternoon when I answered a knock on the door, there stood HIMSELF, the good looking ruffian!

"Oh, it's you," I said. "I told them not to send you!" He turned to leave, but I told him to come in and look at it again.

"It didn't need a new switch at all — I've proved it's simply the catch on the door that is not holding the door tight enough to turn the switch on. I told you that in the first place."

He tinkered for a few minutes with the door catch and after he pulled up a little piece of metal that had slipped down to the bottom of the catch, the thing worked perfectly. I ended up minus fourteen dollars and eighty-six cents for a new switch that I didn't need.

When the suds return on my automatic washer refused to return the suds, I had a man come to check it. It happened to be the manager of the Company. He said it was worn out, removed it, placed it in his kit so that he could order one like it, presented me with a bill for eight-fifty for the service call, which I paid, and away he went. One year later, since I still hadn't heard from him, I called the company, told the man who answered, what had happened, and he said he would look into it. He phoned me later to tell me the suds return wasn't there, and neither was the man who had taken it away! He had left the company and it was under new management.

I got in touch with the manager of the store, where I had purchased the machine, who had told me to get the fellow who had vanished, and he got one of their former repairmen to put my machine back in working order under the guarantee.

We had always prided ourselves in having a dry cellar but one rainy day when I went down to get a nail, I noticed the shelves where we kept the nails, paint, and varsol were wet. I sniffed at the shelves to see if the Varsol can was leaking, but there was no odour. Further examination showed that it was water trickling in from the corner of the fuse box, and the inside of the fuse box was rusted all through. As it was still raining when Clare came home, we could see the water pouring through the conduit over the electric wires.

He heated some tar and put it all around the pipe where it went down into the asphalt driveway. The next time it rained the two-quart tub under the fuse box was half-full of water.

I phoned the Public Utilities Office, told them of our difficulty, and their electrician said, "There is a plate on the pipe that could have become loosened or cracked when the driveway was put in." Once again it was Jim, our son-in-law, to the rescue. He chopped, chiselled, and dug into the driveway until the plate was exposed. Then he covered the plate with some expensive sealer that was guaranteed to do everything but hold back a tidal wave, refilled the "canyon" he made in the driveway, and left for home.

You guessed it! The next time it rained the two-quart tub was almost full! I called the Public Utilities again, two of their electricians examined it, agreed that it was coming in where the wires come in, but they couldn't figure out how it got inside that pipe! Up the ladder one of them went to see if it was following the wires from the top near the roof.

"Seems to have enough of a loop to direct it away," he said, as he removed one of the wires to make the loop bigger.

Then they left, instructing me to let them know if the rain

continued to come in. Once again, you guessed it! The next time it rained the tub had water in it!

Jim came over again, connected the hose to the outside water tap and instructed Clare to spray the water directly onto the lower portion of the electric conduit while Jim and I watched in the cellar. As the water gushed through, he rushed outside, told Clare to turn the water off, wiggled the conduit, and found that the joint about one foot above ground level was loose. Then I rememdered! The men who had covered the house with aluminum siding three years before had bent that pipe away out and pushed it back after they completed their work, and they must have damaged the threads. The water was sprayed on that one spot to make doubly sure the leak was found, and Jim repaired it.

From the time we converted the furnace to oil, when we first moved into the house, we had a leaking oil pipe. I reported it to the Company, they sent a man up to look it over. He put some white material around the joint and left. I hung a can on the pipe to catch the drips! My second complaint brought the man back again. "Awfully hard to stop an oil leak," he said. "Water is a different thing, almost impossible to stop oil seeping through."

Fifteen years later when the oil burner konked out on the bitterly cold March evening that we arrived home from Florida and a new heating system had to be installed in a hurry by a different company, they mended the leaking oil pipe for us, but their tinsmith left us with a leaking water pipe, which he had damaged when he tore out the old cold air vents and a chimney pipe that leaked soot all over my new floor!

Oh, yes, the new floor! That reminds me! Our cellar floor had always been a problem! It simply refused to keep its coat of paint on. The recreation room was easily remedied with wall-to-wall carpet, but that would never do in the other rooms. Picture us sawing wood, metal, shining our shoes, or painting, over a wall-to-wall carpet!

A friend of ours, who worked with Clare at the City Hall, had told us about the modern flooring that could be put down in layers in the cellar or in any other place. "It's easy to clean, no waxing or anything. Just wipe it off with a damp mop. They have it out at Grobe's Nursery just off the Guelph Highway. It's so easy to repair to," he said.

We went out to Grobe's Nursery, took a look, and we liked

the appearance of the floor. "Takes quite a beating out here with all their customers running in and out," Clare said. "It wouldn't get a small fraction of the wear at our place."

My fingers leafed over the yellow pages of the telephone book until I saw the "Modern Flooring" advertisement. Arrangements were made for an estimate. Five hundred and fifty dollars to do the two rooms, which included a two-inch layer of cement in one of them where the floor was crooked. I signed the bill and paid almost half of it in advance.

A week later when the boss arrived with the cement man, I opened the window, fastened it up to the ceiling, the cement man put the shute through the opening and shoved it right through the window pane.

"Oh, I'm sorry, M'am, I'll have that fixed for you," said the boss.

"Don't bother, it's all right," I told him. "I should have told you it doesn't go quite to the ceiling because of the cold-air pipe on the new furnace." (Son-in-law Jim repaired that too!)

The cement floor was laid and a good job they made of it too. Several days later one layer each of sizing, polyurethane, a mixture of gold and green plastic chips, and another of polyurethane, were spread on the floor. I paid the balance of the bill and, as they were leaving, the boss advised me to allow four days for it to set before putting anything back in the room.

Everything from the two cellars had been stuffed into the recreation room and, as we brought the articles out to put them in place, I picked up the weather-beaten, worm-eaten plank which I saw the cement man bring in to support his automatic cement puddler. I almost took off when I turned it over and found that it was alive with woodlice.

I had no idea that the men would bring such a decayed mass of corruption into a house, let alone place it in the recreation room on my new wall-to-wall carpet among the furniture, clothing, and everything. Although it was in there for a week, the woodlice didn't get into the furniture or boxes, but stayed around the floor near the walls and some went up the walls into the ceiling. We sprayed in between the rafters above the recreation room ceiling every evening and every morning we vacuumed dozens of dead ones from the carpet. As their population decreased, we cut down our spraying operations, but we didn't see the last of those pests until six months later. Fortunately, they never got to the main floor of the house.

Three months after the floor was laid, the "easy to clean, easy to repair" flooring came off in patches the size of a dishpan in the room where it was put over the new cement, the man who did it had gone out of business, the material had been removed from the Canadian market by the Government, and we were left holding the bag — of dead woodlice!

In fact, I was so plagued by repairmen, even a trip downtown on the bus almost proved to be my undoing! I boarded it at Sheldon Avenue, sat down beside my friend, Mrs .Pope, and, as we chatted away, a young man boarded the bus at the next stop carrying a heavy parcel about three feet long. As he stopped to take the seat across the aisle, he turned the parcel the wrong way up, and out shot a heavy metal bar that landed on my foot. He didn't say he was sorry, but just glared at me as if I should have had my foot in my pocket!

"What is that?" I grimaced, as he picked it up to replace it in the box.

"It's part of a machine I got repaired for my boss," he said.

"What's your name and where do you work?" I snapped, as I took a piece of paper and a pencil from my purse. "I'll have to show this foot to the doctor. Who knows what might develop from a blow like that!"

He gave me a name and said that he worked for General Springs, and, by that time, the bus was at the street where I had to get off. I hobbled three blocks to the doctor's office on one good foot and the heel of the injured one. It couldn't have happened at a more opportune time because I had an appointment with the doctor and that is where I was headed in the first place!

When I got home, I telephoned General Springs to tell them about it and they claimed they had no such person in their employ.

Chapter XXIII

A Surprise for Uncle Rueben.

Our travelling experiences brought us face to face with a cyclone, a plague of fish flies, a bawdy house, hail stones the size of golf balls, sand crabs, miniature snakes, parrots with roller skates, a smattering of apartheid, and fast-talking real estate salesmen.

It was in June, 1954, when we made our first trip to Lacrosse, Wisconsin, to surprise Clare's Uncle Rueben that we ran into the cyclone, fish flies, hail stones and bawdy house. We did the nine-hundred mile trip in two days and when we were within about twenty miles of Lacrosse where the highway runs along a wide arm of the Mississippi River, the welcoming party greeted us!

The wind was so strong Clare could hardly keep the car on the highway. The fish flies got thicker and thicker until the windshield wipers would no longer operate, and the lights were almost nil. We stopped several times to clean them off, but in a few minutes, everything would be covered again. Since we knew it wouldn't be safe to stop there for the night, we inched our way along, skidding sometimes, from the carpet of bugs on the roadway, swerving from a heavier blast of the wind as it gained momentum. Then, after what seemed like an eternity, as we crossed a long bridge, we saw the glimmer of lights in a high building with the word "Hotel" above the door. The bridge slanted up hill, then down again, and we slipped and sloshed as Clare pressed the accelerator on the upgrade or the brake on the downgrade, but we made it to the parking lot near the hotel.

It was impossible to open the door of the car against the wind on the one side but after Clare slipped out of the driver's side, I wiggled behind the wheel and managed to get out through the same door. We inched our way along toward the hotel door and as Clare hung on to me so that the wind wouldn't blow my ninety pounds up into a tree, we reached the door, tried to open it, but the wind was the winner. All we could do was to bang on it in hopes that we would be heard above the roar of the wind; a man from inside opened the door and helped us to get into shelter.

"Awful night to be out, folks," he said as he motioned to a young fellow to help with our bags.

We didn't have enough breath left to answer him! While Clare registered and paid for a room, I noticed three young women, their faces overdone with rouge and eye shadow, all dressed up in bright chiffon dresses, sitting on a chesterfield at the back of the hallway. For the few minutes we were standing there they glared at us as if we were there to hold up the cashier! We followed the fellow with our suitcases upstairs and down the hall to the last room on the left side and, after he placed our bags in the room, and received his tip, he left us. I saw Clare take a side-glance at the mannequin which was painted up and dressed similar to the three girls downstairs, posing with her jazz-gartered leg outstretched as she held one side of her gossamer red evening dress up to her hip!

We looked at each other as we sneaked into our room and as soon as the door was closed Clare said, "My gosh, this is a bawdy house!"

"Oh, No," I groaned, as I cupped both hands over my face in disgust. "No wonder those girls gave me such dirty looks. They thought I was cutting in on their business! And we can't leave now, just listen to the hail stones hitting the window. They're as big as golf balls by the sound of them."

"No, we can't go out in that storm. The wind isn't letting up either, just look at those trees broken off like stalks of celery. We'll just have to stay here, that's all. We're better to put up with this than to have a tree fall on us or to get clobbered with one of those hail stones," Clare said.

Then Clare went over to lock the door, and when he found that it was broken he pushed the dresser, the chiffonier, and a chair against it. He had just finished getting us barricaded for the night when we heard the giggles of some people coming down the hall. Clare's curiosity getting the better of him, he quickly pulled the barricade back to open the door, just a crack! Not to be outdone, I peeked too, and we saw one of the girls from the downstairs hall go into the room across the hall with a man. Shortly after he had re-barricaded the door we heard more footsteps, more talking and giggling, but we ignored it and decided to try to get some sleep.

Neither of us undressed, nor got into the bed, we just rested on top of bed clothing, and prayed for the storm to abate so that we could get out of there! I slept for a few hours, but in the morning, Clare told me he had stayed awake all night for fear someone should come into the room. (We did have considerable money on us).

We got out of there at seven in the morning without even washing our faces, knowing that we could get freshened up at Uncle Rueben's. After we had breakfast at a restaurant and had made some enquiries as to the location of his street, we arrived there about mid-morning. As we got out of the car, I said to Clare, "For Pete's sake, don't tell Blanche and Uncle Rueben where we stayed."

"Heavens, no, Rueben would have stroke."

We told them we had arrived in the storm late the night before and had to get into a hotel, but they never asked which one and we didn't tell them, but Rueben said, "Oh, boy, you can't drive when those June bugs come over. Why, they've often taken the snowplough out to clear them off that bridge!"

Months later, when I told my brother what we got into, he said, "I've always told you to pick the best hotels!"

As I felt my blood surge to the top of my head, I said, "How the devil do you PICK a hotel on a night as dark as pitch, with your windshield and lights an inch thick with fish flies, slipping on a highway greased with bugs, in the middle of a cyclone?"

Chapter XXIV

Excitement.

It was on the beach in Virginia, where we spent our holidays for two summers, that we were first introduced to sand crabs, mini-snakes and apartheid.

Since the sun was too hot in the daytime, we spent many an evening hour sitting on the sand watching the hundreds of sand crabs popping in and out of their holes. They ranged in size from a thimble to a cup, and their oblong bodies were suspended like hammocks from a profusion of fine arched legs that protruded from all four sides of their bodies and made them look like the carriage the Queen rides in. They were scarey little creatures and one had only to move a finger to send them skittering into their shelters. Their get-away was simplified, too, because, with legs on four sides, they didn't have to turn around to go anywhere; they simply went north, south, east or west on whichever set of legs suited their direction.

Honeycombed with a myriad of colors, these miniature landaus reminded us of our bubble-blowing days when we peered into the bubbles to see the many colors reflected there.

A stroll down the beach showed us that snakes can also travel at high speed, for at every step we took, dozens of snakes, about six or seven inches long, slipped into holes in the sand. They seemed to exist where the sand was packed, but the sand crabs favored the looser type.

It was on these walks that we saw sections of the beach that were fenced off and, on the stores just inside, were signs — "Blacks only", or "Whites only".

It was also on these walks that we came across several lobster kitchens. Since Clare wished to sample some lobster, and since my appreciation of sea food doesn't include the shell type, I simply sat down with him to watch him eat it!

Then in March of 1968, we took a winter holiday in Miami, Florida, and a visit to the Parrot Jungle was a must as far as I was concerned. Clare was tired from swimming, and so he stayed at the motel to rest. The sun was shining — the day was happy — we were happy — two friends and I, as we journeyed jungle-wise.

The parrot jungle was bubbling over with the squawks of two

hundred entertainers, ready and anxious to put on their show. We meandered along the paths observing the tropical fish in the water holes on either side. Gold fish — the size of lake trout — sleeking through the water. Cacti, red and yellow hibiscus, orchids nestling in the crotch of trees, the passion flower, the Bird of Paradise and the palm trees enveloped these happy creatures of the jungle.

The parrot trainer — just as ready and anxious — raised his loudspeaker and announced "Come this way, folks, the show starts in twenty minutes." A light rain fell in the interim and the parrots jumped up and down, flapped their wings and stretched them out into the rain, and their squawks were intensified. We didn't know whether our feathered actors loved it or hated it — they put on a show within a show.

Again the loudspeaker was raised and the announcement blurted out — "The show starts immediately, folks" — and start it did. Our eyes were glued to the antics of those colorful birds as they obeyed the commands of their trainer.

They hoisted the flag, rang the bell, answered the phone, pulled dolls in tiny chariots, ringed pegs with the correct colors — there were red and yellow ones — but they never made a mistake. Not only the ones that were in the act, but those that wanted to be before he was ready for them, put the audience in stitches and the trainer in a frenzy.

He adjusted Goldie's roller skates, and directed her to skate down the special six-inch-wide sidewalk, but half way down she stepped off the walk to pick up a choice morsel to eat. "Get back on that sidewalk, Goldie," he commanded. "Gloria, stop banging your tin cup against the cage. Come on, Goldie, swallow that mouthful and show the folks how you can skate." Goldie did her act — up and down the sidewalk she went. Then the telephone rang! "Answer that for me, Bertha, and tell them I'm not in." Bertha lifted the receiver. "Wok, wok, wok," she screamed into the mouthpiece and slammed the receiver down.

"Now, folks," continued the trainer, as he placed a tiny sulky behind each of two parrots, "Charlie and Jeff will have a chariot race." They picked up the handles with their beaks and as they sped along the raceway, the trainer glanced up at the perch, "Barney," he shouted, "stop nuzzling Gertrude. Isn't anything sacred to you any more? Come on, Jeff, don't let Charlie beat you this time."

As we returned to our seats, after a twenty minute intermission, four ladies pushed in ahead of us to get the ringside seats which we were heading for, and we took the ones behind them. The trainer placed Little Joe on his bicycle to ride the tightrope and then as Tony had the American flag raised half way up the mast, I saw the trainer look up as he yelled, "Not in front of company, Caesar!"

The four women in front of us jumped aside, screaming, as the splash hit the front of their dresses!

"Shame on you, Caesar! Sorry ladies! Don't leave that flag at half-mast, Tony, it isn't that bad!"

It was a side-splitting hour!

We returned to our motel, parked our car and locked it. My husband joined us and the four of us went to a nearby restaurant for dinner. After dinner, we returned again to our motel to spend a quiet evening there with our friends. We could see the manager standing in the doorway of his office gesturing to us to come over his way. His face looked troubled as he said, "Your car caught fire."

"You're kidding," I said, hopefully.

"No, I'm not kidding — it really took fire." With that, a guest in the next apartment stepped outside and joined in the conversation. "No, he's not kidding; I drove in beside your car and as I got out of my car I could smell something burning and the smoke was pouring from under the hood."

"I rushed to the motel to tell the manager. He grabbed some tools from his storeroom and said 'I hope the hood is not the kind that locks' and it wasn't, so he quickly disconnected the wires", he continued.

The manager chimed in. "If it had been locked, we would have had to let it burn, and the two cars beside it would have gone too, and perhaps the motel. By the time the fire truck would get here, there would have been quite an explosion from three gas tanks."

"Thank you so much for your quick thinking. What would cause it to take fire?" Clare queried. "It was the starter-switch; as the key was turned off, the switch continued to spin. It got red hot and set fire to the wires. Don't worry about it," the manager continued, "we'll get a new switch and I can put it in for you." This he did and we were relieved and grateful to him.

We retired to our apartment - the four of us - for that quiet evening. Our thoughts turned again to the parrot jungle and a resumé of the day's experiences there was given to Clare.

A few days later, not to be outdone by the fellow who purchased the Brooklyn Bridge, we negotiated to purchase a piece of Cape Kennedy not far from "blast-off".

We saw three pretty young girls on the beach handing out pamphlets as they said, "Take a tour of Cape Kennedy, folks. No obligation." Then the next day at our motel, the manager handed me a pamphlet as he said "Why don't you folks take this sightseeing tour? There's no obligation. You get your dinner free, and then they show you Miami and Cape Kennedy. I think it must be financed by the City or the Chamber of Commerce."

I showed the pamphlet to Clare and our friends and we decided to take the tour the next day. We were to meet at the most fashionable hotel in the heart of Miama, where dinner would be served, some slides shown of what we would see, and then we would be taken on the tour.

We followed the instructions to the letter, but when we arrived at the hotel, we found that we were the only ones there. We were ushered to the dinner table and soon our host came over to sit with us. We ate dinner, with many a side glance at one another, as our host talked a blue-streak about the advantages of living in Miami, how real estate would soar with the Cape Kennedy development, and then we were suddenly ushered to another suite of rooms on the third floor where another gentleman had the screen and slides set up. By this time, we were on to them but we watched the slides to a conclusion, and then the gentleman who was in our party whispered to us, "I'm going to pay them for our meals and get out of here. I'm not buying property here." But nothing would do with those fellows but to take us ten miles out to Cape Kennedy to show us around, and to have us pick a lot on which to build a new home.

During the ride back to the hotel, we tried to convince them that the only thing we would ever buy there was a motel right in Miami, but since Clare would not be retiring for a couple of years that would have to wait. When we returned to their hotel, we offered again to pay for our meals, but they wouldn't accept the money and we left for our motel.

When we told our experiences to Mr. Smith, he was furious. "I will investigate this with the Chamber of Commerce. They left those pamphlets here to distribute to our guests and they certainly don't say anything about buying real estate or I never would have told you to go."

"Don't worry about it," I comforted him. "We wiggled our way out of it, and the astronauts still have their lift-off site."

"Perhaps this is as good a time as any to get back to Kitchener before we do buy the Brooklyn Bridge, or something else goes wrong with the car," Clare warned me the next morning as we packed our friends, ourselves, and our luggage into our Fury Three.

"Shouldn't have any more trouble with a one year old car that gets all the attention you've given it," I told him, as we waved good-bye to the Smiths and started on our homeward journey.

The trunk was full of overnight cases, train cases, suit cases, the largest of which was bursting with groceries our friends purchased cheaper than they could at home. Inside the car, we were up to our ears in string bags of tree ripened grapefruit and oranges. Every time Clare and I switched seats to take our turn driving, we had to rebuild the load around us, and every time we hit a slight rise in the pavement the hind end of the car hit bottom.

We arrived home in three days and after getting unpacked and settled back to normal, and since Clare thought the car wasn't starting the way it should, he took it to our regular service station to have it checked. He told the attendant about the trouble we had in Florida and that we had just returned that day. "How the dickens you ever came that far with this car, I'll never know! Look at this!" he said, as the wiring crumbled to dust in his hand. "Not only that, they've put the wrong switch in. That switch isn't for this car at all!"

He repaired the car, put it in perfect running order, and when the bill was presented to the Insurance Company, we had quite a controversy with them because part of the repairs were done in Florida immediately after the fire and the whole thing had to be corrected here, but they did finally pay all but ten or fifteen dollars of it.

Chapter XXV

This was our Lucky Year?

One Sunday, in the spring of 1968, we decided to take a drive to London, via the MacDonald-Cartier, (401), Highway. I drove down and, after a look around London, we found a restaurant where we had dinner. We gorged ourselves with tomato juice, pork sausage, mashed potatoes, green beans, lettuce salad with French dressing, rolls, butter, pumpkin pie, and tea. Since I could eat only half a meal, Clare had my salad and dessert in addition to his own. (I tucked my buttered roll into my purse to eat later in the car.)

The traffic was very light on the homeward journey as Clare clipped if off at seventy-five miles an hour, and before we knew it, we had passed by the cut-off just before ours. We hadn't talked very much, just sailed along quietly enjoying the fields, trees, the hepaticas in the woods along the way, and I wondered that day, as I had every time I went that direction, if that farmer ever would have that house lifted out of the hole into which it fell when he had it moved there several years before. I was about to turn to Clare to ask him what he thought about it, when the car took a sudden lurch onto the right shoulder of the road, narrowly missing several posts and the guywire that was between us and a twelve foot drop. As my screams woke Clare, he pulled it back on the highway with such a jerk that it bounced on two wheels almost onto the left shoulder then back again to the right lane where we were in the first place! It was several minutes before I came out of shock enough to volunteer to drive the car the rest of the way home.

At 3.45 in the afternoon of the 9th of May, this same year, our home was struck by lightning! Earlier in the afternoon when I went downtown to shop, the weather was sunny and pleasant, but with my shopping completed, I came out of Goudies store into a teeming rainstorm.

Since my raincoat and rubbers were in the car in the parking lot about three blocks away, I put my coat over my head to protect my precious hairdo and hurried as fast as I could to my car.

Needless to say, one does not have to go very far in a pouring rain to get awfully wet; in fact, I was soaked.

I sat my soggy self on my nice clean car seat and proceeded to drive home. During that drive there were three claps of thunder preceded by very severe lightning, but I didn't feel nervous about it because I had often been assured that one is quite safe from lightning while driving in a car because of the rubber tires.

When I arrived home, the first thing I did was to remove my soaking wet coat and dress and take them down cellar to hang on a clothes line to dry. As I hung them up, my eyes fell on some small bits of paper I had spilled in the corner of the cellar just below the electric meter and fuse box. I started to walk over to pick them up.

Within eight feet of the fuse box, I hesitated. "Will I go back to get the broom and dustpan or will I wait until the storm is over and clean it up with the vacuum cleaner?" I thought.

At that moment of hesitation a cannon-like report and a wide flash of fire hit the floor. This was not a case of "he who hesitates is lost" but rather "she who hesitated was saved." A few steps forward would have put me right in the line of fire.

The electric power went off and so I checked the fuse box to see if the fuses were intact. I sniffed around to see if a fire had started and could detect nothing. Even so, I phoned my husband to come home from his office and when he arrived, we checked our appliances to assess the damage.

The power came on again and we learned that it had been turned off because of the intensity of the storm.

In the living room we found the television condenser strewn across the floor in minute pieces; a new radio was burned to a crisp and the lead-ins from the television tower were completely stripped of their rubber coating, only the very fine wires were hanging there.

Things could have been worse. Of course, they could. So with this consolation in mind, my husband and I went to Minnie's Kitchen to have supper. During the supper hour, I started to feel top-heavy and had to lean on the table for a bit of support. After eating, I started to perk up again and didn't feel too bad. We went home and I retired a bit earlier than usual.

When I awoke the next morning, shock had set in and I called the doctor. His treatment had me back to normal in three days and I thought "God's in His Heaven - all's right with the world."

Monday was washday and everything went along smoothly with the washer and dryer and later in the day I decided to iron. I turned the steam iron on, and "Boom" - it exploded as if it were loaded. Steam hit the ceiling, the iron flew out of my hand. I leaped for the plug and pulled it from the receptacle. (The burn on the tiled floor was remedied later when we covered the floor with wall-to-wall carpet.)

Was this the end of the lightning's rampage? It was - until I turned the kitchen light on the next day. When I pressed the switch a flash of light came down at me like a demon from Mars.

So what! There just isn't anything else that can happen. That must be the end! The rest of the week was quite uneventful and we thought the end of the lightning's path had finally been reached, but just like death and taxes, washdays will come up and once again the automatic washer was set to do its duty. The first tubful went through fine and while the second one went through, I went to the kitchen to prepare dinner.

My sixth sense must have been been serving me well that day for when I went half way down the cellar steps to see if all was well - yes, you guessed it - the recreation room was full of smoke and there was a strong smell of rubber burning.

Fire - help - the telephone - "This is 70 Rosedale Avenue, there's smoke in my recreation room". Two or three minutes passed but it seemed like an eternity - the screech of the siren - the back door opened and in came five burly firemen.

They scattered in every direction - some up to the main floor - others in different parts of the cellar. For a few minutes they couldn't find the source of the fire until one of them laid full length on top of my washer and dryer and sniffed behind them. "Here it is," he shouted, "it's the washer." After disconnecting it and opening the window to let the smoke escape from the house, they explained that the smoke had followed the air currents into the recreation room leaving the laundry room perfectly clear.

The firemen advised a complete inspection of our wiring when they knew that lightning was the cause, and this was done the next day.

I have heard it said that lightning never strikes in the same place twice and I can assure you I want very much to believe it.

One day in the Fall of the year, I decided to have baked potatoes for dinner. It was a little late when I thought of it, but I knew they would be ready in time if I speeded up a bit. I turned the oven on first, then I picked four of the biggest ones I could find in the basket, scrubbed them for all I was worth and put them in the oven on some foil. Later when I opened the oven door at the command of my minute minder, there was a poof - and out shot a spray of mashed potato that pelted me like the winter's worst sleet storm.

There I stood on tiptoe teetering back and forth so that my heels wouldn't go into what was on the floor. My glasses were covered like blinders but I couldn't take them off because my hands and arms were full of potato. Well, to make a long story short, the poem I wrote the next day will perhaps suffice . . . . .

Never Trust a Spud

If you forget to prick your spuds
When you're about to bake them,
I'll guarantee that you, like me,
Will suffer certain mayhem.

On a busy day when I was torn
Between too many vocations;
I put my spuds into the oven
Without those perforations.

I opened the door of the spuds' abode
At the sound of the minute minder;
The potatoes exploded in my face
My glasses became a blinder.

I was covered with potato atoms
From my head down to my feet;
So were the walls, the 'frig., the counter,
And the floor was a slippery sheet.

Where will I start to clean up the mess?
My brain began to mutter;
On tiptoe I stood and grabbed paper towels
To get me out of my clutter.

Disintegrated potatoes dangled in my hair,
In my eyes, in my pockets, in an open drawer;
Where, oh, where, will I start to clean
Unless it's with the floor?

If you forget to pierce those taters
When you're about to bake them,
I'll guarantee that you, like me,
Will suffer certain mayhem.

Chapter XXVI

I Blew the Science of Numerology.

I had always been a devout follower of the Jane Gray programs, both on television and radio, watching her nimble fingers as she made something from nothing. "Don't throw anything away!" she would say, as she held an empty milk carton, or an odd shaped piece of styrofoam in her hand. "You can always make something out of it. Look at the candles we make in a milk carton and this piece of styrofoam will make the base for one of these Christmas trees." Although I had heard her talks about numerology, it wasn't until I received a phone call from my friend Helen Shannon that I decided to send for Jane's numerology chart.

"Jean sent for her own chart and also for mine. Why don't you send for yours? You really can have a lot of fun out of it, Flo," Helen said. (Jean is her sister-in-law.)

Send for mine, I did! (What woman doesn't like to take a sneaking peek into her future?) Busy as I was at the time, I figured out the number of every member of our family and some of my friends, and I analyzed them from start to finish. Since I was a number one and my husband was a three, two things in the chart that stood out in my mind were that — "All the little troubles that had been bugging number ones in 1967 were past, and 1968 would be a much better year in every way," and that, "For the best results, a number three person should always marry a number seven".

In spite of the first prediction, 1968 was even worse than 1967, and so it was suggested many times to me by Mrs. Harold Wagner of Waterloo that I write to Jane Gray to tell her how completely opposite the numerology chart was for me.

"O.K.", I told her. "I'll write her in poem form." The next morning in two hours and a half, this is what developed . . . . .

(To Mrs. Jane Gray - Radio Station CHML - Hamilton, Ont.)

Aug. 15/68.

Your talks on numerology
Aroused my curiosity.
So I sent for a copy of your book
And into my destiny, took a good look.

One thing I learned that sounded great
Was the improvement for me in Sixty-eight.
The demons that plagued me all last year
Had decided to embark on a new career.

I am a number one you see
And my husband is a number three.
Forty years of married bliss we've enjoyed
So you can imagine how I was annoyed.

On studying your numerology chart,
My marriage was wrong right from the start.
My husband's life would have been a heaven,
If he'd only married a number seven.

Those demons left me, the chart says for sure,
But let me assure you, they're still at my door.
Close by me they're bound they will hover around
To weigh my shoulders right to the ground.

They made me break my partial plate.
My diamond ring they seem to hate.
They snapped off the claw, the diamond they broke
And left me with all the expense of that joke.

They got into our heating system, we had no heat at all.
It took a thousand dollars a new one to install.
We thought they now would leave us in sanctity
And your numerology chart would become a reality.

But no, they were not ready for fields afar,
So they decided to monkey with our car.
They chose a spot on highway 401 —
Our new Fury Three konked out like she was done.

A Provincial Policeman was our salvation
And drove us to a service station.
A loosened fan belt the attendant fixed
And we drove away with feelings mixed.

Now would those demons leave us alone,
And strike out for other parts unknown,
And let my numerology chart
Improve '68 after a very bad start?

Oh, no, it would be no use other people frightening,
So they decided to strike our house with lightning.
How they giggled when it ripped us apart
And deafened my left ear, and almost stopped my heart.

Our radio ruined - the T.V. condenser
Strewed across the room like it went through the mincer.
The lead-ins stripped of their rubber coating,
My poor steam iron in its water was floating.

Some of the damage from this event
Didn't show up till two weeks were spent.
I started my washer my clothes to make clean.
The house filled with smoke - the siren did scream.

Five burly firemen hurried my way
And straightened out my troubles, at least, for that day.
I decided then to iron some clothes
But I just brought on some further woes.

I turned on the switch - the iron exploded.
I dropped it quick - I thought it was loaded.
It ruined a tile on the recreation room floor,
And the iron itself would work no more.

We planned on doing the recreation room over -
Painted the walls - the floor we did cover.
On wall-to-wall carpet our money we splurged.
Sunset orange and yellow motif emerged.

The room all splendent like peaches and cream,
It looked just like a young bride's dream,
Till I looked at a monstrous wet spot on the carpet.
Our dehumidifier decided to leak from its sprocket.

Brand new carpet just down one day -
Christened with water so the glue wouldn't stay.
A new hose was procured for the offending machine,
Once again we thought everything was serene.

The lightning's strike nearly got me too.
I was close to the fuse box when it came through.
The cannon-like report deafened one ear.
I was stunned too stupid to have any fear.

Delayed reaction - some call it shock
Set in the next day, and I called the Doc.
Three days later I was all set straight
And waited to see if this would change my fate.

The following week, my fears were real.
My husband decided to go to sleep at the wheel.
Doing seventy-five on 401 highway,
We missed the curve and I sure did pray.

My screams woke him up and he missed posts and wire
By one little inch, which is as good as a mile.
The car went on two wheels, first the left and the right
And, believe me, I prayed with all of my might.

We rented a cottage for the month of July -
Figured on having a restful holiday.
The Hippies on motorcycles took over - we lost -
Our sleep, and one hundred dollars it cost.

We took a trip through Mackinac
To put the demons off our track.
We chose the best motels - high price -
But the demons beat us to it like mice.

They blocked the water pipes up tight,
And put the manager in an awful plight.
They got this repaired at a very late hour -
And then we lost the electric power.

In the morning the guests were all adither.
The ice cold shower sure made us shiver.
So once again we went on our way,
Hoping this would start a better day.

This is only *a few of the things* — I will have to summarize.
They got my ear; they got my teeth; and then they got my eyes;
For I put my glasses on my face and everything looked dim.
Those pesky little demons had broken them at the rim.

My kitchen light shot flames at me
When I turned it on so I could see.
Lightning sure does things so queer;
It filled my ninety-pounds with fear.

Last year in Florida - our car took fire -
Bought a new one so we wouldn't have to hire -
The window of this one disintegrated like peas
And the mirror fell off, narrowly missing my bony knees.

My home was like Grand Central Station
With repairmen to fix my refrigeration.
Self-defrosting the company guaranteed it -
But they forgot to inform the frig. 'ere they freed it.

My ulcers have ulcers riding piggy-back, and I am on a diet.
Six sheets to the wind I would like to get - and I believe I'll try it,
If some kind person will enlighten me -
How to get canned when you only drink tea.

Exaggerations! don't you believe it.
I'll swear it all on an affidavit.
So please call off those little stinkers
Before I completely pop my clinkers.

So Good Luck, Jane, with your numerology,
But count me out as just an apology
For a *number one* that couldn't have been *born,*
But was plucked from a cabbage patch one frosty morn.

Mrs. Florence M. Hammond,
70 Rosedale Ave.,
Kitchener, Ont.
(Born January 28, 1907)

Jane took it like the good sport that she has always been. I knew she would, and I am just as sure that she won't mind if I let you in on the contents of the letter she wrote me by hand in spite of her busy schedule.

Ste 918-919
SHERATON-CONNAUGHT HOTEL
Hamilton, Canada
Thursday

Dear Mrs. Hammond:

Without a doubt, your poem is one of the cleverest I've ever seen! I have read it many times and have shown it to several friends. We all agree that you ought to start sending your work out to magazine editors. It *really* is a gem.

I am amazed that you can write so wittily after enduring so *many* heart-breaking episodes in your life! You are a brave girl and I am dreadfully sorry to learn that so much happened to you in such a short period. I *do* hope and pray that the black days are over.

For some unknown reason, a large number of (1) persons have experienced terrible times during the past two years.

My son, who is a (1) has had the worst year of his career (free-lance artist). After a lifetime of almost perfect health, he has had to seek medical advice for really serious trouble — People died — owing him money — he had *nothing* on his drawing board for months — This has been a very strange year from a Numerical standpoint. A (*6*) year should be a year of peace and harmony and progress! *What* a year it has been!

Directly the '69 Charts are ready, I'll rush you and Helen your copies. And - again - I *do* pray that your "session in the Valley" is now over.

With every good wish. (Signed) *Jane Gray.*

Chapter XXVII

Do-As-You-Like-Day.

At our place, Saturday is do-as-you-like day. An extra hour's sleep helps to start the day off right. No need to get up at seven o'clock on Saturday morning.

But on Saturday, the twenty-eighth day of September, Clare had an appointment at ten in the morning. We arose at eight o'clock, dressed, and he went to the bathroom to shave. I went to the kitchen to prepare breakfast.

"I'll have orange juice this morning, please," were the words floating from the bathroom above the soft music of the living-room radio.

"Breakfast is ready," I announced.

"Be there in a minute," he said.

We sat down to eat breakfast. Orange juice, toast - whole wheat for him - white for me. He had honey with his toast - I had black raspberry jam with mine, the kind that has the seeds removed. Hot tea gave us the lift that lets you stay lifted.

As we sat there relaxing for a few minutes, the air was still reeking with the smell of the toast - my husband likes it burned to a crisp. Woe betide the person who scrapes it!

I cleared the table, placed the dirty dishes in the sink and started to wash them. Clare went to the clothes closet in the hall to get his suit coat and leave for his appointment. I heard the door rattle, the twisting of the knob, then a mumbling voice.

I turned to see what the trouble was. "What's wrong?" I exclaimed.

"The door knob is broken. Look, it just turns around and around and doesn't release the catch," he answered. "Now what will I do - my suits are all in there, my wallet, my car license, everything I need is in there."

I went to the kitchen and got my paring knife out of the cutlery drawer. I inserted the knife into the crack between the door and the door frame and tried to pry the catch out of the hole. The knife just slipped against the catch. Clare nudged me aside.

"I'll remove the pins from the hinges and take the door off." It sounded like a good idea.

"First of all, we must remove the mirror." So we removed the full length mirror from the door and laid it on the living-room rug. He got the hammer and screwdriver and pried and tapped the hinge pins. Finally they loosened, and with that cat-that-swallowed-the-canary look on his face he tried to lift the door out.

"This should do it," he said as he pulled, jerked, and banged it with his fist. But the hinges had been painted so many times that try as he could he could not separate them.

"What can I use to pull the door out that won't damage the paint?"

I dashed to the kitchen and got the gadget I use to pull pies out of the oven. He tried it, but the prongs just bent back with the first pull.

He hurried out to the garage and returned with the wrecking bar and a piece of two by four to rest it on for extra leverage. Then he rushed into the bathroom for a bath towel to protect the floor. The wrecking bar, plus the bath towel, was too thick to go under the door.

Next he rushed down into the cellar to the tool box and came back with an old handle off a barn door. This went under the door but it would not cling to the door - it was too rounded. Into the kitchen he went and came back armed with a rubber spatula and scrubbing brush. The spatula would not go through the crack but the scrubbing brush was too thick to go under the door.

"I suppose as soon as I turn my back the door will probably fall on me," he said as he replaced the pins.

"Just leave it," I said. "I'll call Jim to come over. He might be able to get it open."

I phoned Jim and told him about our plight. "I'll be right over," he said.

"I'm two hours late for my appointment," lamented Clare, as he paced back and forth. Then he darted for the cellar again and came up with a linoleum knife, pressed it into the crack against the latch and, presto, the latch snapped back and the door came open. He grabbed his coat.

"Phone Jim, quick, and tell him it's open. Perhaps he hasn't left yet," chirped Clare. But Jim has already come in our back door, a linoleum knife in his hand.

"It's open, Jim, I got it open with a linoleum knife," my husband beamed.

"There isn't a door lock you can't open with a linoleum knife - even a Yale lock," Jim informed us. "When my brother and I were working on apartment buildings years ago, we often had women cry 'I'm locked out of my apartment and the children are inside, screaming,' and every time, we opened their doors with a linoleum knife."

"I'll come over next week and put a new lock on the door for you," volunteered Jim.

"Thanks, I appreciate that - must hurry - two hours late for my appointment - be seeing you," Clare said as he headed for the back door.

I gazed at the mess - one bath towel, one paring knife, one rubber spatula, one old handle from a barn door, one screwdriver, one linoleum knife, one piece of two by four, one scrubbing brush, one hammer, one wrecking bar, and my gadget for pulling pies out of the oven.

I shook four mats, vacuumed the living-room rug, washed the muddy footmarks from the kitchen floor and stairway leading to the back door. I removed the finger marks from the mirror, from the door and from the framework around the door.

Then I collapsed in a reclining chair and let my mind go blank. This was my do-as-you-like day!

Chapter XXVIII

Work and Play with Group #3

To finish our Church work season for the summer, Group #3 always ends up with a potluck picnic for the June meeting. One of those enjoyable get-togethers prompted me, as recording secretary, to make the following entry in our minute book:

The Fun Group of St. Andrew's called Group Number Three,
Wanted to go on a picnic spree;
The president looked 'round a little discreet,
Mrs. Kopperson suggested 156 Mill Street.

June 19th was the date that was set
And every food came that ever was "ett".
The members came with it in mighty full force
And Boy did we enjoy every course.

The table was set 'neath a big apple tree
And the garden itself was a joy to see.
Each member came with her best appetite;
Diets forgotten at least for that night.

Before we sat down to partake of this food,
We thanked God in song for all of His Good;
Good health, good homes, good friends to enjoy
And peace on earth, we must never destroy.

Our hostess did much this picnic to prepare
With the help of her husband who also was there.
Coffee and tea were his special charge
And he served them with gusto in cups small and large.

Business was dispensed with for this fun meeting
And chit-chat took over and many a greeting.
The big apple tree even took part
By dropping its green fruit to give us a start.

Let's not forget before we go 'way,
That even a little toad had his "heyday"
When one of our members "full of old Nick"
Presented him to many, who withdrew their hands quick.

The gathering ended happy and gay;
A wish from each other for a good holiday;
With rest and relaxing for every one
Till our busy fall season opens up again.

Another feature of our church activities was the annual tea and bazaar which was held in the month of November. We seldom sold every item but one year we had so much left over that the president of our group, Mrs. Verneda Russel, suggested that we rent a table at the Kitchener market and try to clean them out. Everyone agreed and Verneda asked me to help her with the project. Recorded in the minutes is this account of our experiences:

If a Market Vendor You Have Never Been —
Girls You Haven't Lived

You fall out of bed at five o'clock sharp
And down to the Market for a nice early start.
You peak through the slits, where once you had eyes
And spread on the table all your lovely supplies.

The first hour is slow; you sell very little;
Till a neighboring vendor says, "Prices you must whittle".
Away below cost your prices you set
For taking the goods home is a very poor bet.

About nine o'clock, the crowd grows thicker
And the people flock 'round and commence to dicker.
The prices are low, but they want them lower;
Even twenty-five cents seems to make them glower.

So down you cut prices till it hurts you inside;
Saying nothing about injuring your Presbyterian pride.
Customers you can read like a story book;
Whether they're there to buy or just "take a look".

Finally, you sell quite a number of things
And add a little more to Group Three's purse strings.
The work of our Ladies Aid to support
You'd go through most anything without a retort.

To do your bit for the Ladies Aid,
Not an unturned stone would you ever leave.
You'd fall out of bed to the alarm clock's din
And find that your girdle is outside in.

To turn it again and change all that luck
You'd certainly have to have lots of pluck.
Unless you've sold "leftovers" between Frederick and Scott,
Let me tell you, girls, you have missed a whole lot.

Since the president is always looking for ideas to make money for the Church, it was suggested that we have a dessert party. The event was a success for both fellowship and funds and was so recorded:

The Dessert Party

The March 18th meeting of Group Number Three,
Turned out to be a dessert party.
Our members fingers deftly prepared
A table of goodies which was uncompared.

Ladies from all of our Church Groups attended,
And outside churches were represented.
Plates were fill smorgasbord style
As they gazed on the food with a groan or a smile.

They sat down at tables with pretty adornments
Of flowers, serviettes, and other accoutrements,
To indulge in conversation with friends,
And eat those calories till they had the bends.

Behind the scenes the desserts had fun
Telling one another of the work they had done.
The jello shook as it told its vices
And the chocolate cake slipped a lot of its slices.

The pies and whipped cream did the flips
As they bragged about pounds they put on the hips.
Tortes and squares did plenty of braggin'
We made them gain gobs on the part that they're draggin'!

Hairdos and flower arrangements were exhibited
To make our party's success unlimited.
The treasurer collected the shekels we need,
As the president mingled among the élite.

Everyone helped clean up the mess
As to overeating they had to confess.
The Fun Group of St. Andrew's has done it again;
Their dessert party was successful - Amen, Folks, Amen.

Age was no barrier to belonging to our church groups. Our members celebrated tin weddings, wooden weddings, silver weddings, and golden weddings. Mr. and Mrs. J. N. H. McAinsh celebrated theirs at their home on Pandora Avenue, Kitchener, on January 23, 1965, and I wrote the following poem in their honour, framed it in a gold frame and presented it to them that day:

That Golden Wedding Day

Fifty years ago today a very happy pair
Decided to get married — each other's lives to share.
They looked toward the future with faith and trust in God
As down life's sometimes rocky road they went with all their love.

A bountiful crop has been gathered in
As they gleaned the fields of friendship.
Friends they have held all through the years
To share their joys, their sorrows, their tears.

They lost a leaf from their family tree;
She was needed in Heaven more than here you see.
For God was short of an angel up there
To assist with His Work at the Golden Stair.

Their interests wide and varied
Are always mutually enjoyed.
Their Church, their business, their home, their flowers
Keep their busy hands employed.

Honesty and integrity were the basis of this marriage.
Adherence to the Golden Rule they always seemed to manage.
They didn't choose the easy way although it was apparent;
But stood upon their principles and reached their goal inherent.

Many weddings have come and gone;
Paper, Wood, Tin, Silver and Iron.
Now they have reached the Golden One
We wish them many more to come.

Good luck, good health, we wish them today
As they continue down life's "Great White Way".
May their lives be brightened by the friends they have gained
And their faith in the future be sustained.

(Mr. and Mrs. McAinsh were instantly killed in a car accident near St. Marys, Ontario, in 1970.)

The Christmas Party.

Wednesday, the 18th of December, 1968, at 6.30 p.m., was the time set for our Church Group Christmas party.

I phoned Mrs. Fraser. "What time do you think we should get down to the Church - five-thirty?"

"Oh, I think we should go down sooner than that. The ladies will complain that we didn't help them," she answered.

"Well, maybe I had better come right away and we can be down there before five o'clock."

"Yes, I think that would be better."

I left immediately, picked her up in my car, and we got to the Church by five o'clock.

We took off our coats and hats, hung them in the hall, and proceeded to the kitchen.

Mrs. Sisson, President of our group, Mrs. Near and Mrs. Bain were busy cooking vegetables for our dinner.

"Don't put any pepper in the vegetables," I sang out to the ladies. "Several of the members can't eat pepper."

"Oh, we've heard that three times already," snapped Mrs. Near.

Mrs. Fraser and I placed our purses on the unused portion of the counter where the other ladies had theirs and volunteered our assistance.

"There's nothing you can do at the moment — unless you want to check the table to see if the cream and sugar is on."

We went to the Elizabeth Room, accomplished our mission, and returned to the kitchen.

Mrs. Mason was just coming in at the back door. She flopped her heavy basket and purse on the counter as she said, "Merry Christmas, everybody." Then she left the kitchen and went down the hall toward the dressing room.

The hunger pangs in my stomach prompted me to look at the clock. It was six-fifteen.

Mrs. Mason returned to the kitchen. She removed her camera from her bag and focused it on the backs of the ladies working at the sink. She clicked the button but the flash bulb didn't work. She changed the bulb and tried again. The second one failed.

"It's probably the battery," Thelma Miller warned.

"I think I have a battery in my purse," said Mrs. Mason as she turned toward the counter.

"Where's my purse?" she yelled, as she spun around to look in all directions.

Twenty-two of us took up the search. We examined every cupboard, every drawer, the garbage cans, under chairs, every place we could think of.

A voice piped up, "Did you leave it in the car that brought you to the Church?"

"No, I had it after I came in here. I had been out visiting all afternoon and came straight to the church, so I went to the washroom to freshen up and I used my powder and lipstick."

Down to the washroom she darted. A few seconds later she returned.

"No, it's not there." Her hands shook as she again looked around the kitchen.

"How much money did you have in it?" Mrs. Sisson asked.

"Seventy-nine dollars. I wouldn't care so much about the money if I could only get the purse and other things back. Our house keys are gone. I will have to change the door locks."

"Did anybody come in the hall outside of our own group?"

"Yes, two boys went down the hall, and I also saw a strange woman go to the washroom."

Two men entered the kitchen carrying a large roasting pan. It was the turkey they had cooked for our party. They placed it on the counter, lifted the cover to show us how it was carved into servings, and left the church.

The aroma was too much for our empty stomachs. Another glance at the clock - it was seven p.m. Thelma Miller whispered in my ear, "I'm starved - I haven't had anything to eat since noon."

"Better call the police and report the loss of your purse!" Mrs. Near warned.

We straggled to the table a few at a time - some still hovering around in a last effort to find the purse.

Mrs. Mason went to the phone to call the police.

Within ten minutes, two detectives arrived. Shortly after, two uniformed policemen stood in the hall. They talked to Mrs. Mason. I could not hear what was said. They entered something in their notebooks. They talked a bit louder.

I heard one officer say, "We searched outside the Church, but we can't search inside unless one of your Church members goes with us."

Mrs. Mason accompanied them and they searched inside. A look of disappointment was evident as they returned to the Elizabeth Room.

"Let us know if it turns up," one of them said as they left.

"Yes, I will. Thank you very much."

It was after seven o'clock when we sat down to appease our gnawing stomachs. We had turkey with all the trimmings, mashed potatoes, turnip, peas, jellied salads, relishes, cookies and Christmas pudding with hard sauce.

"Who made the pudding? I would like the recipe." Mrs. Withington enquired.

"You can have the recipe if you pay ten cents for it," retorted Mrs. Near, "and the money goes to our group funds."

"Oh, yes, you did that with your Queen Elizabeth Cake recipe, and we collected quite a bit of money."

While we were still smacking our lips over Mrs. Near's Christmas pudding, our President announced, "The dinner will cost each one a dollar. There are twenty-two here. Mrs. Mason gets hers free because she lost her purse." The ladies applauded.

Dinner over, we buzzed around, twenty-two of us ran back and forth to the kitchen with dirty dishes, put left-overs in the refrigerator, washed dishes, dried them, and put them away. Group three upheld its reputation. We left the kitchen spotless.

"Hurry up, girls, Thelma's going to show pictures of her trip to Europe," Mrs. Sisson said.

Thelma led the way to the Heather Room, set up her screen, and we travelled with her through Rome, Vienna, Paris, and up the River Rhine by bus.

Then Mrs. Kirkland, Mrs. McAinsh, Mrs. Fraser and I left for home in my car.

"Isn't it too bad Agnes Mason lost her purse? It cast a shadow over the whole party," I remarked.

"Could have been worse - she could have broken her leg or something," Mrs. Kirkland quipped.

With this philosophical note in mind, I delivered my passengers to their homes, wished them a Merry Christmas, and went on to my own home.

Chapter XXIX

Whiling Away The Time.

It was Sunday, February 15th, 1969, when our friends Faye and Eric were to return to Sault Ste. Marie on the eight-thirty plane from Malton Airport. "Since you've completed your business in Oshawa, how should you like to spend the day in Toronto?" I asked.

"That would be thrilling! I'd like to see the Museum," agreed Faye.

"So should I," echoed Eric.

We had breakfast, packed our luggage, checked out of the motel and proceeded to Toronto. Since it was noon when we arrived we parked the car and went to a nearby restaurant for dinner. As we entered the building, the aroma of roast chicken teased our hunger pangs. We removed our wraps, seated ourselves at the table and learned from the waitress that they served nothing but chickens, quarter chickens, or half chickens, with the works.

"If it's as good as it smells, it suits me!" said Clare.

"Me too!" Eric beamed.

So chicken it was, quarters for the ladies and half chickens for the men, ice cream, and tea.

"Lucky we got a parking place so close to the Museum," Faye groaned as she slipped off her shoes. Should have worn my walking shoes. Look how these are cutting my insteps!"

After dinner, we headed with the crowd towards the Museum. As we entered the hallway, we could see everybody looking at the mosaic dome eighty feet above. Beside us four totem poles reached eighty-six feet, six inches up into the stairwells. We waited in line to take our turn through the turnstile. "How much is it?" enquired Clare.

"Twenty-five cents," returned the attendant.

"I'm paying for four," said Clare as he dropped four quarters into the box and waited for the gate to open!

"Wait a minute! That last one's a nickel," shouted another attendant as he flicked the money back.

"Oh, no it isn't — it's one of those new quarters — I've been fooled with them too, I boasted.

"O.K., go around the outside. They won't open the gate," he said as his face turned red!

As we sauntered around the first floor, our eyes feasted upon the cases of emeralds, diamonds, amethysts; the antique dishes, clocks, incense burners, jewel cases, and ancient statues.

"Let's go up to the second floor! I want to see the dinosaurs," I suggested. The elevator was so busy that we trailed up the steps one behind the other.

"Oh, boy, do my feet hurt! Guess I'll have to take my shoes off," sighed Faye as she turned to a couple of guards. "Is it all right if I walk around in my stocking feet, sir?" she enquired.

"Oh, yes, lots of women do. That's O.K.," grinned the guard as he continued his conversation with his partner.

We entered the room to the right and towering twenty-five feet tall the skeleton of a Duck-billed Dinosaur seemed to be glaring at us. The plaque at his feet revealed that he had roamed the Sand Hill Creek district of Red Deer, Alberta, millions of years ago. Next in line was the skeleton of the Horned Dinosaur - the Giant Centrosaurus Apertus, also from Red Deer, Alberta.

A crocodile that also had lived with the dinosaurs sixty-five million years ago was there. His bones were brought back from an expedition in 1954 from Alberta. His history said his skull is as complete as that of a modern crocodile.

Next we came to the common Iguana from tropical America. They named him "Charlie" because they claim he was a friendly fellow. He has been with the Museum for five years.

"We've seen enough of this room. We're going upstairs," Clare informed me.

"O.K., you folks go ahead. I'm staying here. I want more information about the dinosaurs." The three of them left for the third floor. I wandered to the Dodo skeleton which was found on the Island of Mauritius where they roamed around the Indian Ocean until 1698.

As I stood transfixed before the Devil's Corkscrew, pencil and notebook in hand, two girls, about ten years of age, squeezed in front of me and started to write notes about the phenomenon, the fatter one quite oblivious of the fact that she was standing on my feet. Five minutes later they skipped away to the next point of interest. Having been released from my pinnings, I got the rest of my information about the Devil's Corkscrew.

It appears that these corkscrews occur abundantly in the strata about two hundred feet deep, between the headwaters of the White and Niobrara Rivers in Sioux County, Nebraska. While their origin is not understood, some authorities believe them to be sandfill cavities formed by a plant, while others believe they represent burrows made by small rodents. The latter view is supported by the finding of the skeletons of these animals in the corkscrews. This specimen was twelve feet high and thirty inches in diameter.

A little boy questioned his mother at the next exhibit. "How long is that dinosaur, Mummy?"

"Oh, I don't know. It's pretty long."

"It's forty-seven feet," I told the little fellow as he gazed at the dinosaur.

I felt a tap on my shoulder! It was Eric. "Think it's time we were going. By the time we have supper and get to Malton Airport it will be close to plane time."

The elevators still being jam-packed we trailed down the steps one behind the other and as we were leaving we scanned the eighty-six-foot-six-inch totem poles and the Mosaic Domes towering above our heads.

Chapter XXX

Signs of The Times.

It was a beautiful day that Friday in March, 1969, - cold, but sunny. I waited at the corner of King and Queen Streets for a friend I promised to meet. The street was buzzing with traffic and people were scurrying this way and that. The mini-mall repulsed me with its filth accumulated over the winter months.

Beside me two old ladies lamented about their pensions being inadequate to meet the rising cost of living.

A gentleman hurried down the other side of the street clutching the hand of a little boy about two years of age. The wee chap's arm was stretched to the limit as he galloped along five steps to the older man's one.

The Brink's armored truck stood beside the bank, mostly on the sidewalk. An old man with a very red nose leaned on his walking cane as he examined it.

Men with brief cases rushed in and out of banks and from offices.

Two young girls, loaded with school books, and dressed in mini-skirts that looked more like misplaced cummerbunds sauntered toward the trolley bus. Their mouths were busy on an over-sized wad of chewing gum.

As I looked to the left I saw two people coming down my side of the street, dressed in bright green slacks with gold stripes. Looks like two girls, I thought! No, it's two boys! No, it isn't - it's a boy on the right and a girl on the left! No, it's a girl on the right and a boy — oh, well, it's two people - I think!

Then Margery appeared and I said, "Let's get out of here while I still have my sanity!"

Chapter XXXI

He Served Them Well.

When Clare entered the employ of the City of Kitchener on October 15th, 1935, he told Mr. W. P. Clement, one of the gentlemen who recommended him, that he would never give him cause to regret it. Clare never worked in half-measures, but always set his objectives high and strived to attain them.

As Assistant Tax Collector for twenty-three years and twelve as Tax Collector, he worked constantly to increase the efficiency of the Tax Department in reducing its tax debt and thereby saving the taxpayers the interest it would cost to borrow money.

When he was appointed, about twenty-eight per cent of the city's taxes were overdue or uncollected every year, the worst per capita debt arrears for any Ontario municipality. By 1961, he had reduced the arrears to only about two per cent. and for the last seven years before his retirement, Kitchener had the smallest per capita debt arrears of any municipality.

He was proud of this achievement. To quote the late Rev. Harry Emerson Fosdick, he "found a high purpose and built himself around it". He "gave himself to it with all his heart". He loved his job, but it often necessitated stepping on the toes of some of his associates who had been used to financing their businesses on the lower rate of interest it cost them for holding back their tax payments. This not only gained for Clare the image of one of the toughest tax collectors in the province, but it also dubbed him with the nickname of "Rocky". (Not another name!)

Even though his attitude was tough, there was always a soft spot for the sick and oppressed who couldn't pay. Many a woman had cried in his office over her arrears notice, but she always went out smiling about the arrangement "Rocky" made for her.

"How much could you pay per month?" he would ask.

Perhaps she would hesitate for fear that what she had in mind would be too little.

"Would ten dollars a month be too much for you?" he would suggest.

"Oh, no, we could manage twenty dollars a month. We don't want to get any farther behind."

"O.K. We will make out postdated cheques for twenty dollars

a month and if anything happens that you can't make it one month phone me and we won't put the cheque through," he would tell her.

As he handed the cheques over for her signature, he would say, "I didn't make one out for December, that's Christmas, and you will need it for the family!"

Yes, there was a soft spot! For several years, every time the taxes were due, he would receive a phone call from an elderly lady on Queen Street, South, who was confined to a wheel chair, telling him that she had her money ready. Then he would call there on his way to work at lunch time to pick up the money to pay her taxes for her.

Many times he acted as adviser to married couples who were finding it difficult to pay their taxes and five or six other creditors at the same time. He would advise them to borrow from the bank to consolidate them into one debt and to purchase only the bare necessities until they pulled themselves out of the hole. Later on, one or the other of them would thank him for his suggestion.

The time that a former Kitchener mayor called him to his down-town office and handed him ninety-five hundred dollars in cash to take back to the City Hall to credit against his tax bill often caused Clare to chuckle and me to shudder.

One day a man Clare had worked with years before, in Twin City Signs, came in to pay his taxes and when the clerk charged him a few cents penalty because the bill was several days overdue, he went into Clare's office and said, "Why didn't you phone me and remind me that I hadn't paid my taxes? I thought we were friends!" (Just picture a busy man going through thousands of names in the rolls every day to see if one of his personal friends had had a lapse of memory!)

One Saturday morning he had occasion to go to the office and since he had given our neighbour, the late Carl Seibert, a lift down town, he asked him if he would like to see his new office. As he was showing him around, Carl said, "What's this?" as he put his foot on the burglar alarm button!

In seconds, the police were hammering on the door. Clare opened it and as he turned to Carl, he said "O.K., Carl, tell them what happened!" Red faced Carl explained, and Clare added, "Sorry, Officers, everything is all right, just a mistake."

A born perfectionist and a demon for speed, he always prided himself on the fact that he never lost a dime for the city during all the years he handled cash even though he came close to it the first year he was there. On that occasion he was balancing the day's take of sixty-five thousand dollars and after he flipped away at the coins his total showed a fifty-cent shortage. Try as he liked he couldn't find it and he ended up taking the cash over to the treasurer - short fifty cents. Then, as he was hurrying back to his office, he felt something hit his foot! There was the fifty-cent piece lodged in his wide pants cuff. He returned immediately to the treasurer's office, told him what had happened and gave him the fifty-cent piece.

Even his bad habit of scratching at every blemish that he sees with his index finger paid off during his days on cash. That was the time another cashier was out one hundred dollars and they had almost given up trying to find it, when Clare noticed an amount of one hundred and ten dollars in one column. "That can't be right," he said, as he scratched at it with his over-active digit and removed the leg of a fly that had been carelessly swatted during the day. "I knew that couldn't be one hundred and ten - that's the lady who pays ten dollars a week on her taxes," he said as he pointed to her name.

The co-operation of an efficient staff and, sometimes, the services of a bailiff did a great deal to help him reach his goal. That is when Alan Hamm (Hammy) came into the act. Hammy had been trained as a boxer in his early years so that one look at his strong physique and his determined-looking face often brought a quick settlement when he confronted a tardy taxpayer. But, like Clare, compassion emerged from beneath that tough exterior when he would come face to face with people who simply could not pay.

When Clare retired on June 30th, 1969, he had served under sixteen mayors, the population had increased to four times its size, all hundred thousand of them were his bosses, and he served them well.

Chapter XXXII

Just a New Phase.

Today is Saturday, the twenty-first day of August, 1971, two years and two months after retirement. Retirement — the end? Anything but! To us, it has been the beginning of a new phase. Since there were too many "do-as-you-like-days" for Clare during the first four months, he secured a part-time position as a process server for the Sheriff's office, which took him back on work that has a lot in common with his former position, but with pressure not nearly so great. Since it is a part-time job, he still has time to enjoy an occasional trip, a dip in a friend's swimming pool, an hour's tinkering under the hood of the car, or working around the garden.

For me, there weren't enough "do-as-you-like-days", but I managed to squeeze in a hobby that I wanted to do for years.

I wrote "Little Apples Will Grow Again" and this book is its sequel.

We are both busier than ever, but certainly more relaxed. Several times during the week our only communication with each other is by way of notes left on the kitchen table. "Clare — left at 11.30 — having dinner at Goudies — hairdo at 1.30 — back by 4. Flo."

When I arrived home another note said, "2.45 — popped in — ate ham sandwich and dill pickle — popped out again. C.P."

The day I had to take some books to Guelph, I left a note saying, "11.30 — left for Guelph — back by 3 — The traveller."

The answer — "12.30 ate lunch — appointment at 1.30 in Baden to take another writ to one of my good customers — Traveller #2."

In spite of this busy schedule, there is time for reflection at breakfast time, in the evening, or at weekends. From our back door at seven in the morning, a myriad of colors from the flower bed, which stretches the full width of the garden, gives us the satisfaction of a job well done. As we view the Cornflowers, Zinnias, Four O'clocks, Snapdragons and Carnations arrayed in their vivid pink, white, royal blue, yellow and orange dress, their heads laden with dewdrops that sparkle like diamond tiaras, their feet carpeted in mauve and gold by the Sweet Alyssum and Marigolds, we are reminded of the happy days. But here and there a couple of flowers appear to be in a clinch and closer examination reveals that old Creeping Charlie (wild Morning Glory) has wound itself around them like a rattlesnake, which brings to mind the troubled times when we had to uproot the "Creeping Charlies" from their stranglehold on our lives.

The other day when Clare called me to the door, he pointed to the flower bed and said, "Look over there!" and I saw a hummingbird hovering like a miniature helicopter, drinking the nectar from a flower. This morning, the same thing happened but this time it was a canary. "Don't very often see one of those around here," I said, as I watched it pick the seeds from a dead Cosmos bloom. "Hope that little fellow leaves some seeds for me to plant next year!"

After sundown, the flowers reflect a different picture. The colors are deeper and the damp evening air, like that of the morning, transmits their perfume to our nostrils to tranquillize our weary minds. As I cupped two pink rosebuds in my hands they seemed to be puckering their petals to be kissed like my two granddaughters Cathy and Shannon do when they leave to go home.

A black squirrel and a grey one raced neck and neck across the lawn toward a tree where they seem to have taken up residence.

"Grey squirrels and black ones usually fight, but those two seem to get along fine. They've been together all summer!" I remarked to Clare.

"Yes, I noticed that too, but do you know why they're hanging around here? They're stealing the peaches off Sisson's trees, chewing off the fruit, and then burying the stones in our flowerbed!"

"Nothing like storing up for a hard winter!" I prophesied.

As the chilly night air became more penetrating, and we gathered up the folding chairs to put them in the garage, a piece of white paper fluttered across the lawn in front of us and I thought of that day in the Bank of Montreal back in 1928 when a piece of blank paper determined our destiny.

And so little apples did grow again.